JAPAN AND

HUMAN

SECURITY

21ST CENTURY OFFICIAL DEVELOPMENT

ASSISTANCE POLICY APOLOGETICS AND

DISCURSIVE CO-OPTATION

Otto von Feigenblatt, M.A.

Academic Research International,
1347 D High Point Way, NE
Delray Beach, FL 33445
United States

Manufactured in the United States of America

Second Paperback Edition ISBN: 978-0-6151-7386-3

To my dear fiancée Vannapond
Suttichujit

and to my parents the Baron and
Baroness of Feigenblatt-Miller

ABSTRACT

Japan's foreign policy is often described as abnormal and opportunistic due to its perceived deviation from the norm established by the ruling international relations paradigm, neo-realism. This study concentrates on one policy field of great international visibility, official development assistance. Japan's official ODA policy is taken as a representative example of its foreign policy and serves to test the impact of the rising Human Security Paradigm. This innovative paradigm has been adopted by Japan as a pillar of its foreign policy and its language is widely used in official policy documents. Due to this a discursive analysis was undertaken so as to determine the impact of the Human Security approach on Japan's Official ODA policy and consequently identify Japan's official position regarding this approach.

This dissertation then tests Japan's actual ODA projects planned and implemented by the Japan International Cooperation Agency and the United Nations Fund for Human Security in order to determine whether there is a gap between Japan's version of the Human Security approach and its actual policies regarding ODA. This test is not concerned with the actual results of the projects in question or with their impact on their target beneficiaries but rather with the level of coherence and consistency of Official ODA policy discourse and actual project implementation.

Three main results were revealed. Regarding Japan's official position of the concept of Human Security, its position closely resembles that of the United Nations Commission for Human Security which favors a balanced view of the paradigm tackling both "freedom from fear" and "freedom from want". This approach allots equal emphasis to protection as to long term empowerment and favors a concerted effort by all major stakeholders. In summary this view lies between the Protective Human Security of some "middle powers" such as Canada and Australia and the United Nations High Commission for Refugees and the developmental Human Security of most radical non-governmental organizations and the United Nations Development Program.

The second result is regarding the impact of the Human Security paradigm in Official ODA discourse. It is clear from the detailed discursive analysis undertaken that Human Security has permeated this policy area. Finally the third result deals with discursive co-optation and the forces behind the efforts to mainstream Human Security. This dissertation shows how conservative neo-realist stakeholders in Japan have identified common instrumental security goals with those of Human Security and have co-opted the use of the language of Human Security in order to further the ultimate goal of the "normalization" of Japan in a neo-realist fashion.

ACKNOWLEDGEMENTS

I have acquired numerous debts of gratitude during the process of undertaking the research that led to the present dissertation. Those debts can be divided into two distinct categories, namely those based on instrumental help and those based on inspirational support.

The importance of instrumental help is often underestimated when in reality it is of utmost necessity in order to carry out any academic undertaking. One important instance of instrumental help for which I wish to express my most sincere gratitude is for my parents help in procuring many of the rare books required for the present dissertation. Their patience, dedication, and financial support for the author's protracted studies are greatly appreciated. I would also like to thank my godfather, Phillip von Feigenblatt, for his financial support. Other important debts related to instrumental help are to the MAIDS' staff for their patience and flexibility, to my dear fiancée for her help with the translation to Thai, and to my fiancée's mother, Amornrat Suttichujit, for her logistical support.

Now I will turn to those debts of gratitude related to inspirational support. I would like to express my gratitude to my fiancée, Vannapond Suttichujit, for her constant encouragement and support during the tedious process of undertaking the research for the present dissertation and most importantly for the great meals she prepared for me during the process. I would also like to mention the emotional support provided by my mother and the inspiration provided by all of my professors.

CONTENTS

LIST OF TABLES

Tables   **Page**

LIST OF FIGURES

ABBREVIATIONS

AFP	-	Asia Forest Partnership
AIDS	-	Acquired Immuno Deficiency Syndrome
APEC	-	Asia Pacific Economic Community
ASEAN	-	Association of Southeast Asian Nations
BHN	-	Basic Human Needs
FAO	-	Food and Agriculture Organization
FATF	-	Financial Task Force on Money Laundering
FDI	-	Foreign Direct Investment
GAP	-	Grey Area Phenomena
GNP	-	Gross National Product
GTATM	-	Global Fund to Fight AIDS, Tuberculosis, and Malaria
HDI	-	Health and Development Initiative
HIV	-	Human Immunodeficiency Virus
IAPI	-	International Partnership on Avian and Pandemic Influenza
IGO	-	Intergovernmental Organization
ITTO	-	International Tropical Timber Organization
JICA	-	Japan International Cooperation Agency
MDG	-	Millennium Development Goal
NGO	-	Non-Governmental Organization
NOWPAP	-	Northwest Pacific Action Plan
OECD	-	Organization for Economic Cooperation and Development
PKO	-	Peacekeeping Operation

PKPM	-	Community Empowerment Project with Civil Society
PMO	-	Peacemaking Operation
TNC	-	Transnational Corporation
UNDESD	-	UN Decade of Education for Sustainable Development
UNDP	-	United Nations Development Program
UNFPA	-	United Nations Population Fund
UNODC	-	United Nations Office on Drugs and Crime
WFP	-	World Food Program
WHO	-	World Health Organization
WWII	-	World War Two

CHAPTER I

INTRODUCTION

1.1 Overview

The second largest economy in the world is located in East Asia and has exerted a strong influence on neighboring regions. Japanese economic power saw a sharp rise after the Korean War and the period of high economic growth. Due to Japan's export oriented economy, the government identified early on, that its economic future depended on its ability to penetrate foreign markets and of taking advantage of the natural resources of other better endowed nations. The recognition of those economic imperatives led to the formation of the Japanese trading empire, whose expansion was undertaken without a single bullet being shot.

Due to the strong connection between trade, foreign investment, and economics in general to development, Japan took a leading role in helping Asia, more specifically East and Southeast Asia, develop as potential markets for its finished products and as necessary sources of raw materials and cheap labor. Several tools were used to do this such as official development assistance, foreign direct investment, private loans, training programs, and more recently free trade agreements. All of those tools of foreign policy have important ripple effects for the development of the target countries and because of this Japan had to gradually start to sugarcoat them in its foreign policy discourse in order to justify its economic intervention in them. In other words, Japan had to offer something in exchange to the target countries. The early years of Japan's economic rise after the War lacked any sugarcoating on the part of the Japanese government other than simple trade and free market policies. This started to change after some target countries started to question Japan's policies and whether they were actually benefiting the target beneficiaries or only the Japanese economy. This prompted the Japanese government to justify its policies in order to make them more acceptable for the target beneficiaries. This is when Japan put forward the development argument based on the national norm of "developmentalism" which claims that helping other countries develop is beneficial for everyone not just for the target country. Later on Japan introduced the flying geese model which attempted to justify Japan's economic leadership of Asia by saying that Japan was leading the other dependent economies towards development and economic growth. The period in which Japan took the raw materials from the rest of Asia and then exported back the finished products transformed into a period in which Japan started to face strong competition from other rising East Asian economies and decided to move some of its production to Southeast Asia and China. That shift was also justified at the foreign policy level by the discourse of comprehensive security and international development as a way to help those countries develop and more recently as a way to improve regional and global security. The final step in this process of discourse transformation has been Human Security. The growing popularity of this concept and its all encompassing nature made it a very appealing idea for the Japanese government and was eagerly adopted during the late 1990s. This concept was based on promoting security through development and favored long term solutions instead of short term ones. The nature of the Human Security concept as promoted by the United Nations Development Program (UNDP) fit Japan's "economism" and "developmentalism" perfectly and as another value added consequence it helped Japan justify its lack of military cooperation with the UN.

On the other hand, there are groups in Japan such as NGOs and international civil servants, *inter alia*, who truly belief in the concept of Human Security and think that it is a good framework to guide foreign policy due to its focus on prevention and other dominant development norms such as a needs-based approach. This study will concentrate on the gaps between official discourse and actual implementation of the concept of Human Security.

1.2 Statement of the Problem

It is clear that Japan is making use of the concept of Human Security as the overarching framework of its official discourse. Human Security is used in the most recent diplomatic bluebook to bring cohesion to Japan's foreign policy. The general goal is to give the picture that Japan's foreign policy has the single aim of promoting global human security. Such a praiseworthy goal justifies, at least in theory, all the policies used by Japan in trying to achieve it. When dealing with ODA and development in general, the Human Security approach includes some guidelines for policy making. While the concept still remains loosely defined and flexible, some general characteristics of the human security approach to development can be identified. The first one is its emphasis on prevention and early warning. Long term solutions to root causes of insecurity are preferred over short term fixes. Human Security promotes the use of a holistic approach to development which stresses the interconnectedness of the different areas of security. Two other popular currents in development thinking are also included by the human security approach, namely empowerment, and a rights-based approach. Human Security, especially the version espoused by the UN Commission for Human Security, stresses the importance of ownership and sustainability. Thus the Human Security approach brings under its wings most of the cutting edge development methods.

By claiming to follow a Human Security approach in the promotion of development through ODA and the Fund for Human Security, the Japanese government is making the commitment to follow the guidelines set forth by this approach. This means that the effectiveness and success of its ODA policies will be judged according to whether they help achieve human security or not and whether they follow the guidelines of the Human Security approach to development. This is the main problem that will be tackled. The gap between official discourse and actual implementation and whether following the human security approach makes any difference at all compared to for example following a sustainable development approach. The present dissertation wants to look at how Japan's official adoption of the concept of Human Security as part of its discourse in 1999 has affected its policy towards ODA (MOFA, 1999b). The challenge is to assess the actual effect of the concept on actual policy making and implementation. Due to the all encompassing nature of the paradigm two variables were chosen to represent Japan's development assistance policy, ODA and assistance through the UN Fund for Human Security and the Japan International Cooperation Agency. By comparing official discourse to actual implementation in the previously mentioned areas of foreign policy it was possible to determine the degree of influence the concept actually has on Japanese foreign policy. Finally a simple yet important question is answered. Is Japan using Human Security as a policy advocacy tool in order to hide its national interest? And a more general question is Human Security more than a change of label for Japan's foreign policy?

1.3 Objectives of Research

- To assess the impact of the concept of Human Security on Japanese ODA policy making and implementation.
- To identify the official government position regarding the concept of Human Security.
- To compare Japan's official discourse to actual implementation of ODA policy and assistance through the UN Fund for Human Security and the Japan International Cooperation Agency.

1.4 Research Questions

- What has been the impact of the adoption of the concept of Human Security by the Japanese government on ODA policy making and implementation?
- What is the official government position regarding Human Security especially in relation to development assistance policy?
- Is there a difference between Japan's official discourse on ODA policy and assistance through the UN Fund for Human Security and its actual implementation and if so what is it?

1.5 Hypothesis

I am very skeptical of the actual impact of the adoption of the concept of Human Security on ODA policy making and implementation. While Japan's official government position on Human Security is very similar to that of the UNDP and of the UN Commission on Human Security the actual commitment by policy makers is doubtful. Some of the most prominent conservative politicians in Japan have espoused the term and used it to further very different goals, such as an expansion of Japan's military capabilities. Other large business sectors may use the term in order to expand their business opportunities. Due to the neo-realist inclination of the majority of the members of the Ministry of Foreign Affairs and of the Diet it is very difficult to believe that the real goal behind ODA policy is the achievement of global human security rather than a more narrow national interest. Thus the hypothesis is that the term is being co-opted by powerful policy makers and the private sector in order to promote national and sectoral interests. In addition to that a large gap between discourse and actual implementation is expected.

1.6 Research Methods

The main research method that was used is documentary research. First a historical analysis of Japan's ODA policy was carried out based on official government documents such as the ODA White Paper and the yearly Diplomatic Blue Books. In addition to that other official government statements such as speeches and position papers were used in order to identify Japan's official position regarding Human Security.

A second step was to compare the results of the previously described discourse analysis with that of accounts by policy makers. In other words, official discourse was compared to accounts made by actual insiders but unofficially. This includes the accounts of former prime ministers and bureaucrats of the pertinent ministries. By doing this some of the hidden motifs behind official policies have been elucidated.

The next logical step was to review the accounts given by NGOs and other civil society organizations regarding the actual impact and implementation of Japanese foreign policy in the Southeast Asian region. This served as a counterpoint to official policy statements and helped identify some contentious issues related to Japanese ODA and other forms of development assistance. This was complemented by scholarly secondary sources which analyze the impact of Japanese ODA to this region.

The final step of the methodology was to look at the actual implementation of some representative development projects implemented through the UN Fund for Human Security and JICA. They were assessed following the guidelines set forth by the Human Security approach. A detailed assessment was also done for other projects carried out with the support of bilateral ODA. Analysis concentrated not so much on the actual success of the project per se but rather on the influence of the human security approach on the planning and implementation stages of it.

1.7 Research Scope

The present thesis concentrated on the post Cold War period and is mostly restricted in focus to Southeast Asia. The present study follows the guidelines set by Japan's holistic view of human security rather than the two prevalent versions of "protection" human security and "development" human security. This means that the guidelines that are followed are those set forth by the UNDP and "Human Security Now" (United-Nations, 2003) by the UN Commission for Human Security. In addition to that due to the large scope encompassed by ODA and development assistance in general, this study gives a general overview of the field at the theoretical level and at the regional level while concentrating on a few representative case studies for a more detailed discussion. Finally the Japanese policy making process is a very complex one which involves many actors, societal norms, and structural constraints, therefore it was necessary to concentrate on a few major examples of each rather than try to cover the entire spectrum. This means that the author had to make informed decisions on which are considered to be the most influential agents for a certain policy or decision.

1.8 Significance of Research

Due to the nature of the research in question, the major contribution will be to knowledge. In addition to that this study may also be useful for policy advocacy groups and non profit organizations promoting the responsible and sincere application of the concept of Human Security. By shedding some light on Japan's apparently idyllic ODA policies this study will improve the general understanding on policy advocacy tools and most importantly on implications of a possible shift in *epistemes* as Foucault foresaw or in paradigms as Khun predicted (Dyson, 2003). This study is a practical application of Foucault's process of discourse formation and it will help elucidate the process by which a state guides and creates a new discourse in order for its policies to be judged by it. This is clearly the case of Human Security in which a country that has concentrated on economic growth and development rather than military cooperation has attempted to justify its behavior by supporting a shift in *epistemes* and thus be able to set the rules of the game. While this is not the central focus of this study, the results and observations gained through a focused discourse analysis of Japan's ODA policy may provide some useful insights for the more complex question of the implications of a shift in *epistemes*.

CHAPTER II

LITERATURE REVIEW AND AN INTRODUCTION TO JAPAN'S

DEVELOPMENT

2.1 Literature Review

A good starting point regarding Human Security is the final report of the United Nations Commission for Human Security. This report is called "Human Security Now" and deals with the most important issues covered by the concept. In addition to that the document is an attempt to establish the paradigm as a useful policy-making framework and includes a varied range of policy recommendations dealing with issues such as refugees, development, environmental protection, disaster relief, and many others. Chapter five is especially useful in that it concentrates on issues of economic security and how the concept of Human Security interprets the problems of poverty reduction and economic development (United-Nations, 2003). It is noteworthy that this single chapter includes concepts and approaches as varied as equity, sustainable development, extreme poverty, governance, trade barriers, empowerment, foreign direct investment, and social protection. The sheer scope included by the term economic security makes its detailed analysis in a single chapter impossible and because of this the section of "Human Security Now" dealing with this topic concentrates on how to connect all of those issues with the Human Security approach and sets guidelines to be followed for policy making in those subfields. Thus the main contribution to the field in question is at a macro level that clearly positions other concepts under the rubric of Human Security.

More specifically dealing with the study being proposed, "Human Security Now" is useful in that it provides a clear and organized framework from which to move forward. It sets guidelines and standards by which to judge policies as human security-friendly or not. It is also useful in that it gives a broad yet clear definition of the vague concept of Human Security as espoused by the Commission and other supporters of development based Human Security. The present dissertation will use the guidelines set forth by the United Nations Commission for Human Security as a theoretical framework from which to assess the compatibility of Japan's foreign economic policy, such as official development assistance, loans, foreign direct investment, and trade, with the overarching Human Security approach.

Another general source at the theoretical level is that by McFarlane and Khong. Their study of the historical evolution of the concept of Human Security *in Human Security and the UN: A Critical History* provides a very good overview of the concept and most importantly it puts the development approach to Human Security in context. This study explains how the concept came to be divided into two camps, one promoting a version of human security that emphasizes protection while another one emphasizes development (Khong, 2006). "We see here the crystallization of a division in the understanding of the concept of human security between a development perspective that sees safety from economic threats as an essential aspect of human security and a rights and protection perspective that sees physical safety as distinct from , and prior to, the address of economic problems." (Khong, 2006)

The book covers the most prominent definitions of human security and how they tend to be vague and all inclusive. McFarlane and Khong also deconstruct the concept in order to test it. They point out several important contradictions such as a lack of a direct causality and overstretch, among others. The most important piece of analysis brought up in this study in relation to economic security is the issue of causation and prioritizing (Khong, 2006). The authors argue that economic security as expressed by the Human Security framework, especially the development approach, fails to establish a clear relationship of causation between the securitizers and the referent of security. It must be noted that by labeling economic problems security problems that means that there has to be a threat and a threatening agent. Even if the second condition of identifying the threatening agent is relaxed, it is still very difficult to find a direct causation between hunger, for example, and conflict or between inequity and health. There exist clear correlations between those issues but the missing intermediate step needed to prove causation can not be identified. Thus it is clear by simple observation that regions with problems like famine and deprivation tend to show a tendency towards conflict but that is not the same thing as saying that hunger is the direct cause of that conflict. This is an important weakness in the argument put forward by the development camp of the human security debate. A second problem identified by McFarlane and Khong is related to prioritizing. Security is about priorities, something that is labeled as a security issue is supposed to have some urgency and thus becomes a priority. The problem comes when Human Security attaches the security label to everything and thus everything becomes a priority. This may be useful as a policy advocacy tool in order to compete for scarce resources but it is not very helpful for policy making. In addition to that some branches of the development camp have identified other security fields such as group and community security. This presents a logical problem since Human Security is by definition people-centered and by placing the security label on a group, be it religions or an ethnic minority, you are prioritizing the needs of that group over those of the rest of the population. If all individuals are secured equally, at least theoretically, then there is no need to secure groups which are collections of individuals. McFarlane and Khong recognize that this problem is most salient at the theoretical level and that the contradictions previously discussed seemed to be ignored or simply not perceived by supporters and activists in favor of Human Security.

The final contribution made by McFarlane and Khong is that they discuss the dark side of Human Security. They bring up the topic of policy entrepreneurship and policy advocacy. Human Security is being used as a way to promote a diverse and sometimes completely disconnected set of issues. As previously mentioned, the security label carries a sense of urgency and this can be used as a way to fight for the attention and resources, especially funding, of major international actors, such as governments, intergovernmental organizations, non-governmental organizations, etc. Interest groups, mostly policy advocacy groups, fight to put their issues on the international agenda and one way of doing this has been using the security label and thus connecting issues previously considered to be part of "low politics" to the "high politics" of international security.

Another study at the theoretical level that was reviewed is that by Paris (Paris, 2001). His study of the concept human security as a viable paradigm is very useful in that it places the concept in the security field. In other words it compares the scope of the concept of Human Security to other fields in security studies. Paris criticizes the all-encompassing nature of Human Security and its ambiguity regarding the identification of a securitizer. After a detailed analysis of Human Security, Paris summarizes his argument by means of a diagram which represents the field of security studies. The conclusion of this study is that Human Security is not a real paradigm but rather an appropriate label for those security studies dealing with non-conventional threats and alternative visions of security. It is important to note that most of his arguments coincide with those of McFarlane and Khong while Paris ignores the possible use of human security as a policy advocacy tool.

Hough's recent book on global security is worthy of mention since it takes an alternative view of security as its starting point. *Understanding Global Security* includes a large section on economic threats to security and subsections on food security, economic sanctions, and modernization, among others (Hough, 2004). It is also noteworthy that economic security is considered by the author as equally important to other forms of more conventional security. Hough also does a very good job in connecting economic security to other fields of security in order to give a better view of the interdependent nature of security. In relation to the present study the most useful part of the book is that which deals with the perceptions of the dominant schools of international relations regarding economic security. Hough discusses how Marxists, economic liberals, and mercantilists deal with economic security (Hough, 2004). This understanding is useful as a theoretical starting point in order to understand the motifs behind the decisions of policy makers of the Liberal Democratic Party in Japan, and those of NGOs and other civil society actors.

In order to get a clear idea of the impact of the concept of human security on other related fields such as conflict resolution it was necessary to review a source dealing with the major trends in this field. Ramsbotham's *Contemporary Conflict Resolution* was very helpful in this respect (Oliver Ramsbotham, 2006). This study connects the early origins conflict resolution to those of peace studies and most importantly to those of the concept of positive peace. The previously mentioned concept has a lot in common with human security and substantive rights. Those similarities have greatly influenced the development of conflict resolution and slowly this has led to an emphasis on deep prevention and long term solutions to the causes of conflict. The influence of human security can also be seen in the emphasis placed on prevention and long term peacebuilding. As Ramsbotham *et al.* states "third-generation peacekeeping can be understood as a component of a broader and emancipatory theoretical framework centered on the idea of collective human security, in turn situated within emergent institutions and processes of global cosmopolitan governance" (Oliver Ramsbotham, 2006). This study is important and useful in that it depicts how the human security approach is actually being implemented and also served as a guideline to judge how ODA for peacebuilding and conflict prevention is being used.

On a more regional level several sources were reviewed so as to get a clearer view of some of the issues related to human security in the Asia Pacific Region. *Common Security in Asia New Concepts of Human Security* (Chen, 1995), *Promoting Human Security in APEC*, and *Asia's Emerging Regional Order: Reconciling Traditional and Human Security* all fall into this regional category. The first is useful in that it shows the early origins of the concept from the older concept of common security and raises some important concerns in the region. The collection of position papers in this edited book represent a range of views regarding Human Security and attest to the vague and contested nature of the concept in Asia. Some of the most significant conceptual debates revolved around the issue of group and individual rights. Chen's article is especially useful as a conceptual guide to what is covered by human security (Chen, 1995). In terms of the present study the most useful piece of information from this study is that related to Japanese ODA during the late 1990s. "Incorporating the argument for political conditionality that ties economic aid to democracy, Japan in 1992 made clear in one of the four principles of ODA that "along with the promotion of democratization in developing countries and efforts to introduce market-based economies, sufficient attention should be paid to the creation of conditions that secure basic human rights" (Chen, 1995). Keizo Takemi's paper on Japan's perspective on Human Security gives a good overview of some of the contentious issues that could be encountered when dealing with its neighbors such as ODA conditionality and the promotion of a free-market (Chen, 1995). The second study dealing with Human Security and APEC deals with the point of view of Japan's neighbors, mostly ODA recipients (Patcharawalai Wongboonsin, 2006). The interesting thing about this study is the clearly different view it takes on human security. This is evident in that the papers included in this edited book tend to emphasize group and community security over individual security and human rights (Patcharawalai Wongboonsin, 2006). Some issues are raised about the dangers of neo-liberal policies and the economic insecurity they can create. This is very important when dealing with Japan and its ODA and investment policies in the Asia Pacific region and more specifically in Southeast Asia. This study was used as a starting point so as to understand some of the negative effects of Japanese ODA and investment policies in Southeast Asia from the point of view of those states. The third source under this regional category deals with the meeting point between Human Security and conventional security (William T. Tow, 2000). This is very important in a region that still values conventional state security above all else and thus finding a meeting point between the two of those views is a good starting point towards gradually moving to a more human security friendly approach. Chen's paper is especially useful in this respect since it covers the difficulties in Asianizing the concept of Human Security. Chen stresses the fact that most Asian states zealously guard their sovereignty and reject any kind of intervention be it economic, financial, or military. According to Chen this was clearly seen when Thailand promoted the concept of "flexible engagement" with Myanmar in ASEAN and this was rejected by Malaysia and Indonesia as not following the ASEAN way (William T. Tow, 2000). This small step towards Human Security was rejected by the majority of the members of ASEAN which shows that implementing a human security approach in Southeast Asia is a very delicate and problematic task. The present study took this into consideration when analyzing Japan's ODA help to this region.

Another necessary level of analysis when trying to understand Japan's human security policy, especially that related to ODA and the UN Fund for Human Security, is that of the normative national level. In other words, this level of analysis tries to understand the major social norms present in Japan which may in some degree influence its perception of the concept of Human Security. A good start in this respect is provided by Dore's study on Japan's internationalism (Dore, 1997). This is a major social norm in Japan which favors a UN centered foreign policy. Dore traces this to the end of WWII and the resulting aversion of war by the Japanese public. This anti-militaristic ethos then placed the burden of security on the United Nations and the hope that global common security could be achieved. Dore is extremely optimistic about the benefits of a UN centered foreign policy but at the same time includes the views of Japanese intellectuals who differ from his views. Some of the great problems in Japanese society are covered by his book such as Japan's place in the world, participation in Peace Keeping Operations, and the kind of role Japan should play in the Asia Pacific Region. The major contribution to the proposed thesis is that it deals with a usually ignored aspect of foreign policy, social norms. Social norms are especially important factors when dealing with Japanese foreign policy and most importantly with ODA. Dore includes the results of several opinion polls so as to support his observations about Japanese public opinion that show a growing internationalism among the general population. The general observations and some of the opinion polls he includes in his study were useful so as to explain why the Japanese government and the majority of the population believe in the necessity and primacy of ODA as an integral part of its foreign policy.

Trinidad's quantitative analysis of Japan's ODA disbursement patterns in Southeast Asia provided a very useful starting point regarding macroeconomic trends (Trinidad, 2007). The methodology used in Trinidad's study was mostly quantitative and included such things as analysis the composition of aid packages to members of ASEAN. The analysis included a look into the proportion of grant aid compared to loans disbursed to Southeast Asia. In addition to that Trinidad also took into consideration other factors such as the political stability of the target beneficiary and the level of economic development. Trinidad's analytical framework revolves around the twin strategies of "spending" vs. "earning" through the use of ODA. He contends that Japan has historically followed an "earning" strategy while several recent trends reveal that its policy is moving towards a "spending" strategy. One of the important observations made by Trinidad is that historically Japan's ODA policy was the result of a balancing of power between the Ministry of the Economy, Trade and Industry

(METI) and the Ministry of Foreign Affairs (MOFA) (Trinidad, 2007). Trinidad contends that the former was dominant during most of the second half of the twentieth century while MOFA started to gain primacy after the Gulf Crisis. METI promoted the "earning" strategy while MOFA favored the "spending" strategy. In addition to identifying the previous ministries as mayor forces behind the use of ODA, Trinidad also claims that domestic pressure favors the "earning" strategy while the international community favors the "spending" strategy. It is clear that while Trinidad's dichotomies facilitate understanding they tend to oversimplify Japan's ODA policy. First of all, it is not always clear how to divide "earning" from "spending" strategies when dealing with ODA since some strategies may have an "earning" potential in the mid and long terms. In addition to that Trinidad makes the logical fallacy of equating "spending" with humanitarian concerns. This is not always the case since a "spending" strategy may have as its goal the increase of a state's relative power in the international system of independent nation-states or the protection of a favorable balance of power. In other words, it is overly simplistic to equate one with the other. Even assuming that the parallel is appropriate, Trinidad's cold quantitative methodology provides mixed results. His correlation analysis of the disbursement of ODA in Southeast Asia compared to GNI per capita provides two main results. Most ODA is still devoted to strategic states such as Indonesia and economically important ones such as Thailand (Trinidad, 2007, p. 111). The increase in loans to Vietnam shown by Trinidad's study can simply reflect the country's economic potential in the eyes of Japan. Finally, Trinidad predicts that Japan will continue to move towards a "spending" strategy based on humanitarian concerns and human security. The present dissertation will attempt to complement Trinidad's study with a much need qualitative aspect and a detailed discursive analysis in order to contradict his prediction.

The second step towards a better understanding of Japan's view of Human Security is that of secondary sources dealing with it. A good starting point was Wah's article on Japan's movement towards human security (Wah, 2003). This article gives a very optimistic view of Japan's foreign policy regarding this new paradigm and traces Japan's early moves to support it. It concentrates on Japan's role in establishing the UN Commission on Human Security and its Fund. The article also stresses the pivotal role played by some Japanese nationals such as former Prime Minister Obuchi and Sadako Ogata present co-chair of the Commission for Human Security and former High Commissioner for Refugees. The article gives a very superficial rosy picture of Japan's Human Security centered foreign policy but provides a good starting point regarding the general characteristics of this approach.

Hook's detailed analysis of Japanese foreign policy was the next logical step so as to understand some of the more technical aspects of Japan's foreign economic policy. Her account of Japanese foreign policy proved to be useful in that it covered major issues systematically, deconstructing them into structure, agency, and norms. While those divisions are artificial they are very helpful in understanding the diverse set of constraints and opportunities involved in Japanese policy making. She also gives a brief account of Human Security but tends to avoid using this paradigm as the central part of her argument, probably because of the loose and vague nature of the concept. However she does mention that it could potentially become the core of Japanese foreign policy (Glenn D. Hook, 2005). Hook also gives a very detailed account of how Japan uses its economic power as an important diplomatic tool and how this takes place in a very organized and planned manner. Her careful analysis of Japan's ODA policy was very helpful for this thesis.

So as to understand the importance of agency in Japan's policy-making process two other secondary sources were reviewed. The first is that by Togo. As a long time member of the Ministry of Foreign Affairs he gives an insiders view of Japan's policy making process. It is also interesting that as a former diplomat he stresses the importance of ODA as a diplomatic tool for Japan (Togo, 2005). Togo also gives a very good account of the conflicting views over ODA held by different government ministries and their respective roles in coming up with a cohesive foreign policy. As a neo-realist, Togo tends to imply that Human Security is mostly used as a policy advocacy tool in order to further national interests. This is important in that he gives a very different picture of the reasons behind ODA compared to that of official government statements. His account will be used by this study in order to try to understand the impact of Human Security on Japan's ODA policy.

A similar account of Japanese foreign policy can be found in former Prime Minister Nakasone's recommendations for the 21st century (Nakasone, 2002). This book is a combination of policy recommendations and of Nakasone's personal views on how Japan went about making policy. His insider account of foreign policy making during the late 1980s is very useful when it comes to understanding the motivations behind the use of ODA by the ruling Liberal Democratic Party. In addition to that as a member of the Diet Nakasone continues to be a part of the policy making process in Japan and thus has a very clear idea of the way in which his fellow diet members view ODA. It should be noted that Nakasone also considers ODA to be an important part of Japanese foreign policy and recommends that it should continue to be an integral part of it. This study will be useful in the proposed thesis as a way to discern the true reasons behind the use of ODA and also some of the interest groups and factions involved in the process of allocating ODA.

Once one has a general idea of Japan's foreign policy regarding Human Security and ODA it is necessary to go into more detail and look at the official stance of the government regarding these issues. This is done by reviewing official government documents such as official statements and government reports. This is an integral part of the present thesis which concentrates on the distance between official discourse and actual implementation. The starting point when it comes to foreign policy is the diplomatic Bluebook. This gives a general account of Japan's foreign policy divided by regions and issues. The latest edition available to the public is that of 2006. Four chapters are especially pertinent for the proposed thesis. The introduction gives a general overview of Japan's general foreign policy goals and policies. This chapter summarizes some major trends in economic policy and also mentions the importance of human security (MOFA, 2006f). The second chapter deals with Japan's regional diplomacy and includes the section on Southeast Asia. This section covers Japan's trade and ODA with those countries and how it fits in the general diplomatic goals set by the government. In general as expected from a government report, it gives a very optimistic overview (MOFA, 2006d). Finally the most important chapter dealing with ODA is chapter three. This section provides a detailed account of the amount, distribution, and goals of the ODA given by Japan. For the present study on Japan's ODA and Human Security this was very useful when dealing with actual figures and their distribution. The report also tries to provide an explanation of why the government allocated that ODA and how it was supposed to be used (MOFA, 2006e). A complementary chapter is that on Human Security. This section tends to be very general but tries to connect other policy areas to the concept of Human Security. Thus it is very helpful in discourse analysis since it provides the justification of actual policies like ODA using the Human Security framework (MOFA, 2006b). A related source is the web page of the UN Fund for Human Security (MOFA, 2007). This Fund was established by the Japanese government as a channel through which it could promote the human security approach. Japan is trying to channel funds through this Fund and thus to justify its support for this paradigm. The web page has a good database of projects implemented by the Fund and a short explanation for each on how the human security approach was applied. Therefore this web page can be considered to be an important source of official discourse at the international level and as a way the Japanese government is trying to achieve greater visibility and mainstreaming for its view of human security.

Another set of sources is that dealing with official statements or speeches delivered by prominent members of the Japanese government on issues related to ODA and Human Security. One example is a speech given by the Japanese Minister of Foreign Affairs Taro Aso on Japan's economic diplomacy (Aso, 2006). In this press conference Minister Aso gives an overview of how Japan uses economic tools to further its diplomacy. Aso also attempts to give rational reasons for the use of ODA as a diplomatic tool and stresses the importance of doing so with clear goals in mind. In other words he states that ODA should be the means not the ends. This kind of policy position paper is very useful for the proposed study because it represents the government's official discourse and sets the standard against which actual implementation will be measured. Another similar example is that by Ambassador

Yukio Takasu dealing with Japan's position regarding Human Security, and more specifically with attempting to find a clear definition for the concept (Takasu, 2006). The Ambassador of Japan in Charge of Human Security states Japan's position on this issue as one that stresses the necessity to keep the concept broad and flexible and to concentrate on furthering its implementation rather than on reaching an agreement on a common definition. This official government statement is useful for the proposed study because it helps assess and identify Japan's position regarding the contested concept of Human Security.

At this point it is important to explain the results of the literature review. In terms of the issue in question of Japan's official discourse on Human Security and its implications on ODA, there is clearly no study in this area. Most studies tend to concentrate on the concept in general and do not go into its actual implementation or lack of it. In addition to that another gap is that no studies have been encountered which assess the gaps between discourse and implementation especially regarding the human security approach and ODA.

2.2 A Brief Overview of Japan's Development

In order to understand Japan's present we must look back. Development is a process that does not happen in a social and historical vacuum. Thus, several present tendencies and characteristics of Japan can be traced back to important historical events. One of the most important of those is that of Japan's peculiar form of Internationalism. This concept is very important since it directly influences perceptions of peace and more broadly the field of Conflict Resolution. In addition to that some of the strongest forces behind policy formation are societal norms. In the case of Japan there are some important norms that come to mind such as "developmentalism", "economism", "pacifism", "internationalism", and "historical guilt". In addition to those basic Japanese societal norms there are other very important historical factors that must be taken into consideration in any analysis of Japan's foreign relations. One such factor is the nature of Japan's post-war development experience. This is a very important factor when trying to understand why Japan followed the path it did and it also helps explain why Japan acts in certain ways in the international stage. In other words, in the same way the individuals are shaped by their experiences, communities and societies are also influenced by what Carl Jung called their "collective unconscious". There are a few theories in social psychology that apply basic rules of the behaviorist paradigm to society as a whole. They include "archetypes" and meme theory. While they present some differences they have one important thing in common and that is that the rules of behaviorist learning through experience can be applied to society. Japan's post-war experience was unique to say the least. The country went from imperial greatness to poverty and destruction. Japan became the first and only country to suffer a nuclear a attack and then was reconstructed by what were considered by many to be "merciful conquerors". The international community, especially the West, gave its support for the rapid reconstruction of Japan. Finally, Japan found itself as the first non-western country to achieve economic development. All of those important events shaped Japan's collective personality and thus a detailed look at Japan's history, especially development history, is necessary in order to understand Japan's behavior towards ODA and foreign policy as a whole. The question then is how far back is it necessary to look in order to have a clear idea about Japan's development? There is no clear answer to this. Some scholars claim, especially economists, that one must look at Japan's Post-war period as a starting point. Historians usually tend to include so many factors that they end up looking back as far as the migration to Japan by the Yamato people. In this study, we will take a middle point, the Meiji Period (1868-1912) (Olenik, 2005).

The Meiji Period was the beginning of a new era in Japan. It was the end of the feudal period and the beginning of the drive to catch up and compete with the West. The young leaders of the time quickly dismantled feudal states and other traditional institutions in order to mobilize the entire nation towards industrialization. The parallel is amazing when one compares this period to the occupation and the early post-war period. Another important point is that Japan adopted a constitution for the first time in 1889 (Olenik, 2005). Patrick Smith describes this period as one of profound change and expectation (Smith, 1997). Japan was on its way to joining the Western Power in the imperial project. In other words, the governing elite decided that it was time for Japan to open up to the West and to try to compete with it. The philosophy behind this parallels that of post-war Japan, in that the goal was adopt Western technology but at the same time to keep the spirit behind it Japanese. This concept was partly embodied in the catch phrase of the time: *fukoku-kyohei*, "rich country-strong army" (Olenik, 2005). From a policy perspective the most important reforms during this period dealt with the centralization of the bureaucracy and the establishment of the Imperial Universities. This was the birth of Japan's *iron triangle*, the bureaucracy, the government, and business. The three cooperated for the industrialization of Japan building modern railways and factories. It should be noted that Japan's government at the time was the guiding force of the project and that consensus and cooperation between the three ends of the iron triangle were expected at every stage. The model that was followed at the time, was that of Prussia, guided by Prince Otto von Bismarck.

Another important event of the era was Japan's invasion of Taiwan and Korea and finally gaining control of the former from China. Japan also signed a security treaty with the United Kingdom and joined the allied side during World War I. After the war Japan was allowed to keep the former German colonies in the region as mandates. This is important because Japan became the first modern non-western empire.

This period was followed by an interesting interlude, that of the Taisho democracy. This period which lasted until 1926 was marked by an increase in democratic practices. Elections were held and a certain amount of civilian control took place. Political parties developed and more debate and discussion was present than ever before. This improvement was dependent however on the wishes of those holding real power behind the scenes. This led to the rapid militarization of the pre-war period.

Many factors led to this. One of the most important ones was the rise in nationalism at home and the power vacuum left by a weak China. In addition to this Japan needed raw-materials for its industries. As a country poor in natural resources it was compelled to buy them abroad. This made Japan very dependent on external conditions. This was specially the case with oil. At the time Japan bought most of its oil from the United States, as Japan expanded its empire to Southeast Asia and other regions the United States and it's allies started to protest and threatened Japan with cutting off supplies. This was considered to be an important threat for the survival of Japan. This same question of getting enough raw-materials and natural resources has been the question that has plagued Japanese development since its beginning. The answer provided at the time was war and the foundation of the Asian Co-prosperity Sphere. This was Japan's attempt to build a sphere of influence such as that enjoyed by the United States in the Caribbean at the time. The Japanese leadership wanted to secure access to badly needed resources. This attempt is also significant in that it shows Japan's ambiguous position towards the rest of Asia. At the time Japan viewed the rest of Asia as brothers but somehow inferior brothers who had to be liberated for the good of Japan. This explains in part the atrocities committed by Japanese troops during World War II. Three important events to note here are the use of thousands of comfort women to entertain troops during the war, the treatment of Koreans during colonial times, and the rape of Nanjing.[1]

The war eventually drew to an end with the dropping of the two atomic bombs in Hiroshima and Nagasaki. This event is probably the most important factor in explaining Japan's present day Internationalism and Peace movements. In 1945 Japan surrendered and General Douglas McArthur started reforming Japan. An important event that occurred at the time was the Emperor's speech over the radio. He declared that he was not a god. Thus in 1946 Hiroito became the first emperor to be considered officially human. This was the beginning towards a drive away from nationalism and the decoupling of religion and state.

The occupation period was a very important one for the modern development of Japan. General Allied Headquarters set about to rebuild and reform the country.

---

[1] Note: This period is very important when trying to understand Japan's human rights record and its policy of low profile.

The early years of the occupation are especially important. Several reforms were introduced. The education system was reformed in order to eliminate some of the previous practices of indoctrination and emperor worship that took place before the war. Land reform was introduced and large states were broken up and the land was given to small farmers. This controlled civilian unrest and made more land productive. Land-lords were compensated and went on to invest that money in industry. This was one of the most successful reforms introduced. From a social point of view General McArthur had the following idea of Japan. "Measured by the standards of modern civilization , they would be like a boy of twelve as compared with our development of fourty-five years" (Smith, 1998). This is what McArthur told the senate in 1951 about the state of Japan at the time. This reflects the asymmetry which lasts to this day in most of Asia between social and material modernization.

 Another important aspect was the introduction of the Peace Constitution of 1947 and its historic Article 9 which renounces the sovereign right to wage war as a diplomatic tool. This was originally strongly supported by the United States in an effort to prevent the pre-war militarism from ever happening again. The constitution was basically drafted by American advisors with heavy input from McArthur himself. However the draft was submitted for approval to a group of Japanese law-makers in other to guarantee support and compliance from the public. The constitution declared that power resided in the people not the emperor and that the emperor was merely a symbol of the unity of the people. This is very important since it set a strong base for Japan's democratic future.

Nevertheless, the most important single article of the constitution is Article 9.

"CHAPTER II: RENUNCIATION OF WAR

Article 9:

Aspiring sincerely to an international peace based on justice and order, the Japanese people forever renounce war as a sovereign right of the nation and the threat or use of force as means of settling international disputes. 2) In order to accomplish the aim of the preceding paragraph, land, sea, and air forces, as well as other war potential, will never be maintained. The right of belligerency of the state will not be recognized" (Japan, 1946). This article has become the center of debate over Japan's foreign policy. The significance of this Article will be explained at a later section of this paper but it is important to note that this restriction limited Japan's options in term of foreign policy.

As the Cold War was beginning, the United States, changed its policy towards Japan. They needed Japan as a strong ally against the communist block and because of this the process of breaking up the huge business conglomerates was abandoned and other equally important reforms such as the purge of former war-time bureaucrats was also discontinued in favor of a more pragmatic approach. "The Reverse" course intended to help Japan industrialize as fast as possible in order to support the United States in the region.

This was initially done through import-substitution and strong protectionist measures. The United States allowed Japanese products access to its market while American products did not have access to the Japanese market to the same extend. This unequal relationship was very beneficial for Japan and in a single decade the period of reconstruction was over. It is important to note that Japan also received a lot of American aid and its economy got a boost during the Korean War. Japan supplied most of the equipment used by the American army in this war due to logistical reasons.

Japan then continued its shift towards an export-oriented economy. The growth experienced by Japan in the post-war period was exponential. The average growth rate from 1950 to 1965 averaged 10 percent annually. The growth in GNP is equally impressive. In 1946 the GNP was of $1.3 billion and it kept rising until in 1968 it reached $167 billion (Olenik, 2005). This unprecedented growth brought many changes to the island nation. Japan was an industrialized nation by the end of the 1960s.

The 1960s and 70s were marked by a "low-posture" diplomatic stance. This was promoted by Premier Ikeda Hayato (1960-1964) (Olenik, 2005). Japan's diplomatic stance reflected both internal and external conditions. The United States had signed a security treaty with Japan right after the end of the occupation and thus had taken the responsibility of protecting Japan and the region from communism. In addition to this, Japan wanted to concentrate on economic growth under the umbrella of the American army (Aoi, 2000). The implications of Japan's "low-posture" diplomatic stance will be discussed in detail in later sections, for the time being it will suffice to say that Japan was reverting to its 1880's policies. During this time the iron-triangle of the bureaucracy, government, and business was firmly established and was to remain the single most important power arrangement until it began to crumble in the late 1990s.

Japan faced some unrest in the 1970s due to the automatic renewal of the U.S-Japan security treaty and due to some of the externalities of economic growth. This was the time of the student protests and also the rise of the environmental movement in Japan.

These two issues will be discussed in greater detail at a later time but it should be noted that the 1970s were a very important time in policy making. In 1972 Okinawa was returned to Japanese control by President Nixon.

This period also saw a growing trade tension between the West and Japan. The growing surplus in trade was starting to affect the West and in addition to that, Japan's protectionist policies were considered to be unfair. This is the period when the Japanese auto-industry rose to world prominence. Japanese business practices also became famous for their efficiency. Fordism gave way to Toyotism. All of these successes helped Japan reach its peak by the end of the 1980s.

The 1990s were not as successful for Japan. The reasons for this are many but one of the most important ones is that Japan was forced to lift its protectionist barriers to trade. This took away Japan's trade advantage over the West. Increasing competition from the West was made even worse by the rising Tigers in Asia. Japan found itself having to outsource some of its production abroad due to wage differentials. This shift in policy came to its climax in the 1997-1998 financial crisis. The same practices that had been praised as the reasons for Japan's economic success were now blamed for its failure. Globalization was changing the rules of the game and Japan's rigid system based on the iron-triangle seemed incapable of coping with the new conditions. This led to a swift change in direction. The Liberal Democratic Party started to promote neo-liberal policies such as deregulation and privatization in order to cope with the global market. This new policies have been able to stabilize the economy but have had many negative social consequences such as rising unemployment and rising insecurity.

2.1.1   A Historical Overview of Japan's Post-war Foreign Policy

Japan's foreign policy has been shaped by its experience during and after World War II. Japan's emphasis on economic security arguably led to World War II and has been an important driving factor behind its post-war foreign policy (Smith, 1997). Japan has very limited natural resources and the process of industrialization made matters even worse since fuel and other natural resources become increasingly important. Thus Marx's historical materialism may provide a satisfactory explanation for Japan's pre and post war behavior. In addition to that, Japan was the first modern Asian empire and thus it had the experience of a colonial power. During this time Japan's role in Asia was very ambiguous. Japan wanted to join the West in terms of technology and imperial power but at the same time it realized that culturally and geographically it belonged to the East. This paradox was evident during the War. Japan presented itself as the liberator of Asia from Western imperialism while at the same time imposing its own imperialism. One good example of the ideology of the time is presented in the classic animated movie *Momotaro's Sea Eagles* and *Momotaro's Divine Sea Warriors* (Feigenblatt, 2006, p. 3). The previously mentioned propaganda clips were commissioned by the Ministry of the Navy in 1944. They both had a similar story line in which the Peach Boy had a group of friends, animals. The Peach Boy represented Japan and the animals represented the rest of Asia. The Peach Boy and his animal friends had to fight against the evil Western Powers. In a moving yet disturbing scene Momotaro teaches his animal friends how to speak by singing the famous AIUEO song. The message is clear. The group of animals and Momotaro represent the East Asia Co-prosperity sphere. The hierarchy implied in the relationship is also evident. Japan is supposed to lead its inferior Asian brothers against the Western Imperialists. Thus the tone was set for the events that came about during the War. Non-Japanese Asians were thus dehumanized and great injustices were done in the name of defending Asia. A clear example of this ambiguity was Japan's role in Indonesia. Japan invaded the former Dutch colony with the excuse of liberating the fellow Asian country from European domination. However, the short lived period of co-operation between the Japanese conquerors and the Indonesians soon became a standard relationship between that of conqueror and conquered. The Japanese used the rhetoric of Asia for the Asians while at the same time subjecting their fellow Asians to their rule and using them for strategic reasons. This ambivalent colonial experience explains Japan's post-war relationship with Indonesia and the rest of Asia for that matter. While Japan used language that empowered fellow Asians to rise against the West, it also subjected them to incredible suffering. Some of the atrocities still remembered by the rest of Asia are Japan's use of forced comfort women and the many massacres such as the infamous "rape of Najing".

Another important factor in Japan's history was that defeat was very traumatic. The end of the war was marked by the use of two atomic bombs and an equally traumatic event, the presence of foreign invaders in Japanese soil. Needless to say, those events were very shocking to Japan and led to a period of deep reflection (Olenik, 2005; Smith, 1997; Togo, 2005). Japan had to redefine its place in the world and most importantly had to come to terms with its actions during and before the War. In addition to the previously mentioned issues, there was another very important one related to the treatment the defeated empire was to receive from the victorious allies. The Japanese were surprised to see how merciful the conquerors were and while there were obvious selfish reasons behind their actions it was undeniable that Japan received a lot of help from the international community for its reconstruction (Olenik, 2005; Smith, 1997; Togo, 2005). As was already described in a previous section of this dissertation the American occupation brought about many changes in Japanese society but the most important aspect was that Japan's ability to defend itself was left mostly under the responsibility of the United States. The previously mentioned experience led to placing Japan's faith in the United Nations (Dore, 1997). The common security provided by the international organization became one of Japan's pivotal norms in international relations.

Now let us look at Japan's postwar reconstruction and reparations. This is very important because it became the blueprint that Japan was to follow for its own ODA. After the War, the United States became the most important provider of ODA to Japan (Togo, 2005). ODA at the time was provided for two main purposes. The funds provided by the Government and Relief in Occupied Areas was meant to be used to tackle immediate needs (Togo, 2005, p. 318). This included humanitarian aspects such as providing food and medicine. Concurrently the Economic Rehabilitation in Occupied Areas provided funds for longer term development. The funds provided were used to secure needed raw materials and other aspects of industrial production. The aid provided by the United States from 1946 to 1951 amounted to around $2 billion (Togo, 2005, p. 319). Japan decided that it was better to repay the aid provided by the United States and it was repaid by 1973.

By the end of the occupation Japan was receiving aid through the World Bank. Japan received aid from 1953-1966 for 33 projects. The total aid received amounted to $863 (Togo, 2005, p. 319). Most of the funds were used for large infrastructure projects such as the first *shinkansen* and dams. Other projects were used for industrial infrastructure that later on became the foundation of Japan's rise to industrial greatness (Glenn Hook, 2005; Nakasone, 2002; Olenik, 2005; Togo, 2005). Thus Japan received aid for both immediate needs and for long term development. This explains Japan's emphasis on a twin track approach to ODA. In addition to that Japan realizes the importance of the aid it received for its economic success. It was only natural for Japan to apply the lessons learned from its own experience to its own ODA to Southeast Asia and the rest of the world.

Finally, it is important to note that Japan has always placed an emphasis in Southeast Asia for ODA purposes. This is due to several obvious reasons. First of all, there is the aspect of geographic proximity. Second there is Japan's need for natural resources and more recently cheap labor. Finally, some of those countries control important trade routes which are vital to Japan (Trinidad, 2007). In other words, there are several geoeconomic imperatives for Japan's emphasis on Southeast Asia. There is another important aspect that is that related to cultural affinity. This factor is more debatable since even Japanese anthropologists and sociologists do not agree about where to place Japan from a cultural perspective (Duckitt, 2000).

In summary all of the previously discussed factors must be taken into consideration when analyzing Japan's ODA policy to Southeast Asia. Japan's foreign policy has historically being UN centered, shaped by the norm of "historical guilt", and finally has placed emphasis in East Asia. All of those factors both enable and constrain Japanese policy making and implementation.

CHAPTER III

JAPAN AND HUMAN SECURITY

Before discussing Japan's ODA policy by itself it is necessary to look at how Human Security is being used by Japan as an integral part of its overall foreign policy. Human Security is a very broad framework and can even be considered to be an international relations paradigm and therefore it is difficult to understand the full implications of its application for ODA policy without first taking a look at how it is being implemented by Japan in other policy fields such as the environment, health, grey area phenomena, and in an important international forum. In other words, this chapter aims to give the reader a bird's eye view of Japan and Human Security before going into greater detail in the following chapters for the field of ODA policy. This chapter will provide the necessary background in order to understand the context behind the discursive analysis of the following chapters.

3.1 Japan's Role in Promoting Human Security in the United Nations

Japan played a pivotal role in the rise of Human Security in the United Nations. The name that comes to mind in this field is that of Sadako Ogata. The President of the Japan International Cooperation Agency and former UN High Commissionaire for Refugees, Sadako Ogata, and Professor Amartya Sen became co-chairs of the UN Commission on Human Security. This commission was established after the recommendation of the Japanese Government in 2001 (United-Nations, 2001). However, Japan's interest in Human Security can be traced further back to Keizo Obuchi, who served as Foreign Minister during the late 1990s. This coincided with the Asian Financial crisis of 1997 and 1998. Former Foreign Minister Obuchi decided to establish a Trust Fund for Human Security in the United Nations. By the time Obuchi announced this plan in Hanoi, he had become Prime Minister and was trying to lead his country out of the crisis. At that time Japan pledged 500 million yen (Wah, 2003). The funding continued to increase during the following years and by 2003 it had reached about $172 million. Japan's role as one of the main donors in the field of human security will be described in more detail in later sections specially concentrating on Official Development Assistance (ODA) and actual projects.

Japan's role in promoting Human Security in the United Nations is not confined to funding. It has also promoted support for Non Governmental Organizations and Grass Root level initiatives. In this way, Japan is implementing the participatory and empowering aspects of Human Security. Some specific examples of this include the establishment of a Human Security fund specifically for grassroots organizations in order to promote an alternative way of intervention, both humanitarian and development related.

In the field of more conventional international security or what Human Security calls conflict situations, Japan has started to play an increasingly important role. Post-conflict reconstruction such as in the case of Cambodia was one of the first times in which the Japanese Self Defense Forces got involved in Peace Keeping Operations (PKOs). Japan has also shown more willingness to get involved in international Peace Making Operations (PMOs). The case in point is that of the War on Iraq. Japan was present in rear operations cooperating with Aegis-class Destroyers. Regarding the field of reconstruction, Japan organized a Conference of

Reconstruction Assistance to Afghanistan in 2003 (Wah, 2003). This shows that Japan is willing to become a more active player in the conflict field.

In summary Japan has been one the strongest supporters of the Human Security framework in the United Nations System. Japan is part of the Human Security Network, which is led by Canada and is made up of 13 countries that support the framework. At this point it is important to note that Japan officially declares Human Security to be a "pillar of its diplomacy" (MOFA, 2006b). In order to conclude this brief introduction to Japan's contribution to Human Security in the United Nations System it is important to mention the latest trend. Former Prime Minister Koizumi applied the framework to the war on terrorism in a speech he gave at the International Symposium on Human Security held in Tokyo in the year 2001 (Koizumi, 2001).

3.2 Japan's Internationalism and Its Implications for Human Security

Internationalism is a philosophy usually connected to what are currently called "middle powers" (William T. Tow, 2000). However this philosophy does not only apply to states. On a more human level it is closely related to cosmopolitanism and a kantian globalism. In other words, it deals with a feeling of belonging to the international community. It includes concepts such as "good global citizenship" and global regimes. One of its most important characteristics is that it serves as a counterweight to nationalism.

Japans' Internationalism is not one that came about endemically. The reasons of this should be evident when considering Japan's history. The end of the war was a traumatic experience for Japan. It was forced to go from an ultranationalist military empire to an internationalist pacifist democracy. The previously mentioned shift was partly externally imposed and partly due to self-reflection. One important speech related to this was that given by the Emperor in which he declared that he was not a god. This was the end of ultranationalism for the time being. Nevertheless a new ideology was needed and this was supplied by the United States. The new constitution was filled with democratic ideals of freedom and liberty. Power was declared to emanate from the people and not from the Emperor. These ideas were eagerly adopted by most of the population due to the hardships they had experienced during the war and the leniency of the conquerors. Massive re-education campaigns, during the first part of the occupation, tried to teach the masses the meaning of peace and democracy.

Due to the circumstances in which Japan was reopened to the world, the new internationalism was one of atonement and guilt. Most Japanese felt that they had suffered a lot because of misguided nationalism and especially because of the armed forces. The outcome of this is that while Japan wanted to be a "good global citizen" it did not feel it had the moral right to be too active internationally, thus the "low-posture" stance. Historical guilt is the distinguishing feature of Japanese internationalism (Smith, 1997).

Japanese Internationalism has started to change and now is shifting towards a more active role and a rising nationalism. Historical revisionism is becoming more common and has raised concerns in the region. Most Japanese feel that their country should play a more active role in international affairs and that the war ended a long time ago so they should move on to become a "normal" country.

In summary Japanese Internationalism has gone through a long evolutionary process. It started as an imposition and as a rejection of the status quo to one in which national and personal pride could be achieved by helping attain a higher goal, global peace and security. In other words, Japan's role is becoming more and more active while its internationalism changes from that of a defeated nation with a tainted past to one of an active "middle power".

Table 1. The Changing Context of Security

Dimension	Old	New
Protection	Territory	People
Threat	Military	Multiple
Institution	Nation-State	International/Local
Policy Framework	Cold War	Comprehensiveness, complexity, and linkages

Note: Adapted from Chen (Chen, 1995).

3.3 Japan's Environmental Policy and Human Security

Japan's cultural background is one that stresses harmony with nature. This is an integral part of Shinto and Buddhism. Nevertheless this benevolent attitude towards nature slowly shifted to a more western one of control over nature. The previously mentioned transition was gradual but became more obvious during the post-war period. Japan wanted to re-industrialize as fast as possible and therefore it set as its guiding principle, economic growth. The 1950s and 1960s were the golden years of GNPsm and saw Japan rise to prominence as a global industrial power. The price paid for this rapid growth was the degradation and pollution of the environment. Japan's coastline was polluted by industrial waste, the cities were covered by a dark mantle of smock which only disappeared momentarily after a heavy rain. Children started to suffer from respiratory problems and others from more serious afflictions such as genetic defects. The causes for those diseases varied from case to case but they all had something in common, they were all related to pollution and the degradation of the environment.

A good example of environmental degradation and population during the golden years of GNPsm is the Minamata disease. This disease was first discovered in the town of Minamata in Kumamoto Prefecture, Southern Japan. In 1956 the first case was reported to the Japanese government. After careful investigation at the behest of the villagers, it was determined that the cause of the disease was mercury poisoning. Apparently a factory owned by Chisso Corporation was releasing toxic waste to the ocean. The waste contained high levels of mercury which were then absorbed by shellfish. In turn, those shellfish were consumed by the inhabitants of the area. The disease causes a serious problem in the nervous system and can lead to paralysis or even death. The importance of this case is that it shows the lack of regulations at the time concerning the environment and pollution. In addition to this, this case was instrumental in raising public awareness in the field of environmental protection.

Minamata Disease is one of the four major pollution diseases in Japan. The other three are: Niigata Minamata disease (mercury poisoning), Yokkaichi Asthma (sulfur dioxide and nitrogen dioxide), and Itai-itai disease (cadmium poisoning). Most of the previously mentioned diseases rose in the 1950s and 1960s ("Four Big Pollution Diseases of Japan," 2007). The four major pollution diseases led to many suits being filed against the government and against corporations. The cause was taken up mostly by women and it is significant in that it is one of those few times in Japanese history in which policy has been promoted from the bottom-up and not the other way around. The issue was concentrated around the concept of *kogai*, environmental disruption. The ensuing campaign led to the convening of the famous Pollution Diet of 1970. Two major actions were taken by the government at this point. The first was to pass Japan's first environmental law. The bill banned "the emission of materials harmful to human life". The punishment for doing so was set to three years of prison (Olenik, 2005). The second action was to establish the Environmental Agency of Japan in 1971. It is important to note that this agency was recently upgraded to full-fledged Ministry of the Environment in 2006 ("Ministry of the Environment of Japan," 2007).

The beginnings of environmental policy in Japan are a good example of the Human Security framework in action. It was a policy originally mostly supported by women at the grass roots level which then was taken up by the government and ultimately by the entire country. In a sense it was a way to respond to people's needs and the government recognized the importance of protecting the well-being of the individual as a priority. The previously mentioned change in attitude led to the creation of the concept of "net national welfare" in order to replace economic growth as a national goal (Olenik, 2005). This transition was gradual and is still in progress.

Taking into consideration Japan's experience with environmental degradation and pollution, the Japanese government decided to promote sustainable development in other countries as a way to help them avoid Japan's mistakes. Japan has taken the lead in environmental issues at the international level for many reasons. One of the most important ones is that the environment is not a very controversial topic and therefore Japan does not have the problem of its historical guilt such as with issues of human rights. In addition to this, Japan is one of the major international donors. This means that Japan has a pivotal position in the field of development.

It is important at this point to describe the ways in which Japan has taken the initiative in the field of environmental protection. In the field of environmental education, Japan was the country that originally proposed to the United Nations the declaration of the United Nations Decade of Education for Sustainable Development (UNDESD). This decade began in 2005 and has as its main purpose the promotion of environmental education and raising awareness on environmental issues (MOFA, 2006b). Japan has also actively promoted the protection of forests. Japan sponsors two organizations against illegal logging, the International Tropical Timber Organization (ITTO), based in Yokohama, and the Asia Forest Partnership (AFP). In addition to supporting civil society organizations in this field, Japan has shown its political will to fight against this practice by advocating the use of only legal timber by G8 countries. This issue was brought up by Japan at the Gleneagles Summit (MOFA, 2006b).

Japan has also contributed to environmental protection by its creation of the 3R (Reduce, Reuse, and Recycle) approach. This is basically a plan of action for a "Sound Material-Cycle Society". This plan of action was at the center of the Gleneagles G8 summit and the purpose of this plan was to promote "economic competitiveness whilst decreasing environmental impacts" (MOFA, 2006b). In addition to that Japan is a signatory and one of the main supporters of the Kyoto Protocol which was adopted in 1997. The Japanese government has tried to strengthen the Protocol by requesting informal cooperation from the United States. This is an important role that Japan can play in the future and has already played in the past. That of a mediator between the East and the West and as one of the closest allies of the United States it is in a good position to promote environmental issues through informal diplomacy rather by than by the more formal Kyoto Protocol or other conventions (Aoi, 2000).

One of the most promising areas of human security is that of disaster reduction. This is an area in which Japan has been very active due to its experience with disasters and due to its advanced technology. Japan is a country prone to great earthquakes and tsunamis. The UN World Conference on Disaster Reduction was held in Kobe 2005. This conference took place after a major earthquake off the coast of Sumatra and the devastating tsunami in the Indian Ocean.[1] The conference led to the drafting of the Hyogo Framework for Action which was then summarized in the Hyogo Declaration. This framework for disaster prevention was supported by representatives of 168 countries and stressed the importance of prevention in dealing with disasters. This reflects the human security framework in that it stresses the importance of the individual, since disasters are not limited to single sovereign nations, and that of prevention instead of simply humanitarian response in the aftermath of the disaster. Japan also supported the creation of a tsunami early warning system for the Indian Ocean in order to prevent the massive loss of lives seen in the last tsunami.

Environmental policy is a field in which Japan is truly applying the human security framework at home and abroad. It is also a field in which Japan has complemented its traditional security framework with that of human security. A prominent role can be observed in that Japan included environmental assistance as part of its effort to help reconstruct Iraq. Environmental policy is a field in which the Self Defense Forces can take an active role while avoiding controversial issues. The Military has the skills and the resources to make a big difference in environmental protection in conflict and post-conflict situations. It is also an integral part of the human security approach to deal with conflict situations to include the environment as an integral part of human security. By taking action at the right time in preventing

---

[1] It is important to note that the conference marked the 10th anniversary of the Great Hanshin-Waji Earthquake

environmental disaster in conflict situations several negative effects can be avoided such as massive migration flows due to environmental degradation, and the pollution of necessary resources such as fresh water. This helps the affected populations recover faster and protects a strong base for development. Therefore environmental protection as that shown by Japan since 2004 in Iraq is a key meeting point between the two views of security. An expanded conventional security framework that included non-state threats and that of a moderate human security framework can lead to the better use of valuable human resources such as the military. Due to Japan's present restrictions on its Self-Defense Forces this is a field in which Japan can take the lead and set an example for the rest of the world. As Lorraine Elliot has argued, human security and conventional security should complement each other instead of operating as separate fields (William T. Tow, 2000).

An interesting initiative promoted by Japan is the Northwest Pacific Action Plan (NOWPAP) which was established in 1994 by Japan the Republic of Korea, the People's Republic of China, and the Russian Federation. The main purpose of this Plan is to protect the environment in the Northwest Pacific area. This area is an important trade route and especially important for the shipment of oil. This has raised fears of possible oil-spills in the already polluted area. The Plan has organized many activities in order to protect the environment in this area such as clean-up campaigns and has supported several NGOs and grass-roots groups. The significance of NOWPAP lies in that it deals with an area full of territorial disputes. Most disputes are centered around natural resources. The three main territorial disputes in that area are the following: the Senkaku Islands between Japan and China, the Tok-to (or Takeshima) between Japan and Korea, and the Northern Territories between Russia and Japan. The importance of these disputes should not be underestimated. The area is considered to be rich in resources such as oil and natural gas which are vital for the economies of the countries in contention. It has proven virtually impossible to settle the disputes using conventional diplomatic means usually backed by military might while a human security approach has proven to be more effective. This is where the NOWPAP comes in. The Plan includes the joint "development of oil and natural gas in the waters off the eastern part of Sakhalin Islands" (MOFA, 2006b). In addition to that the coverage of the anti-spill plan was expanded to included contentious areas such as that of "offshore Sakhalin and the Sea of Okhotsk" (MOFA, 2006b). NOWPAP is based on collective action and cooperation and has helped to put aside the issue of sovereignty in favor of a more human and nature centered approach to environmental protection and resource management. Thus, NOWPAP applied the human security framework to an issue usually covered by conventional security and solved it without resorting to threats or military action.

A proper discussion of Japan's environmental policy would not be complete without mentioning a few outstanding problems. Lately there have been two main issues for which Japan has been criticized on environmental grounds. The first is the continued use of disposable wooden chopsticks. This may seem inoffensive but it is one of the main sources of demand for wood in Japan. The Japanese government has usually tried to brush off the accusation by mentioning that the use of wooden chopsticks is part of traditional culture. The actual environmental impact of the use of wooden chopsticks is still unknown however it is easy to see that around 126 million Japanese using disposable wooden chopsticks daily has an effect by greatly increasing demand for wood usually from Southeast Asia.

One of the most emotionally charged environmental issues related to Japan is that of whaling. Japan is one of the most important consumers of whale meat in the world. It is possible to find whale meat sold in Japanese markets even though it is technically illegal. However there is a loophole in the law regarding the hunt of whales. Commercial Whaling was banned in 1986 but the International Whaling Commission allows the hunting of whales for experimental purposes (Greimel, 2007). Japan has used this excuse for deploying one of the most advanced whaling fleets in the world. The explanation given by the Japanese government is that the activities carried out by this whaling fleet are important for collecting data for the future protection of whales. This explanation does not cover the fact that all of the whales are then sold for human consumption but at least helps Japan keep face. The controversy over whaling has come to light again due to the confrontations between environmental groups such as Green Peace and whaling ships such as the Nisshin Maru. The previously mentioned ship recently went on a hunting mission to the waters near Antarctica and went back to Japan with a load of 508 whales which were then immediately sold for consumption (Greimel, 2007). The real reasons behind Japan's reluctance on abolishing whaling not only *de jure* but also *de facto* are cultural. Whale meat is a highly priced delicacy in Japan. While whale meat is not for everyone, based on the author's own experience, it is a rich source of protein and fat which explains why an island nation whose main protein source is fish would value it so highly.

In conclusion, Japan has learned from its mistakes and has adopted a human security approach towards environmental issues. This is a field in which a "middle power" such as Japan has a key role to play. By applying a human security approach

Japan can avoid many of the difficulties it finds with conventional security such as disputes over territorial sovereignty and the use of its own military forces. It seems that Japan has taken an early lead in this field and has been able to capitalize on its strategic position as the second largest economy in the world and one of the closest allies of the United States in order to promote its human security agenda in the fields of environmental protection, resource management, and disaster prevention.

3.4 Japan's Health Policy and Human Security

Japan is known for its excellent health insurance system. This system provides coverage at a national level and allows Japanese citizens and residents to receive medical service both in public and private hospitals. It is beyond the scope of this paper to go into detail regarding the structure of the national health insurance plan but it should be noted that Japan has attained one of the highest life expectancies in the world, 81.25 years average life expectancy at birth. In addition to that it has a very low HIV/AIDS adult prevalence rate, 0.1% (Central-Intelligence-Agency, 2007). In general Japan is an example of an effective health policy at a national level. Among the few health threats that Japan has experienced in the last decades is that of avian influenza. The outbreak of this disease in Asia in early 2006 was promptly identified as a serious health threat by the Japanese government. This is a clear case of a threat to human security which had transnational dimensions.

The avian influenza pandemic hit Asia in the year 2005. The disease spread at a very fast rate and was a cause of great worry for the region. The nature of the vector was also a surprise and raised fears of "new strains of influenza that are transmissible from human to human" (MOFA, 2006b). The possibility of an influenza pandemic in the region led to the establishment of the International Partnership on Avian and Pandemic Influenza (IAPI) in September 2005. In this case the initiative was taken by the United States but Japan closely followed in supporting the Partnership. Japan organized several conferences bringing together a varied range of stakeholders. One of the most successful ones was the Japan-WHO Joint Meeting on Early Response to Potential Influenza Pandemic which was held from January 12 to 13, 2006 (MOFA, 2006b). The meeting came up with a plan of action to tackle a possible influenza pandemic in the region and at the same time pointed out the transnational nature of this threat to human security by promoting the allocation of funds to developing countries as a method of preventing an outbreak. This is a great example of Japan applying the human security framework to an actual health threat. Japan brought together all stakeholders to discuss the issue and came up with a plan centered on prevention not only on protection. The previous view was clearly stated by Japan's donation of US$155 million to developing countries in the region (MOFA, 2006b).

Regarding the three major infectious diseases, HIV/AIDS, tuberculosis, and malaria, Japan has advanced the Health and Development Initiative (HDI). This initiative follows a human security approach in that it stresses the importance of improving health conditions while simultaneously promoting development. This multi-track approach follows the recommendation of the UN Commission on Human Security which stresses the interrelationship between development, health, education, and other forms of human security (United-Nations, 2003). Japan has pledged over $5 billion in support for this purpose over a period of 5 years. On another front, "Japan hosted the High-Level Forum on Health Millennium Development Goals (MDGs) in Asia and the Pacific in June 2005" (MOFA, 2006b). The previously mentioned initiative shows that Japan is taking a leadership role in the region in order to promote the millennium declaration goals.

On a macro level Japan is also supporting the Global Fund to Fight AIDS, Tuberculosis and Malaria (GTATM). Japan is an active founding member of the Fund and also one of its main donors. Japan has contributed a total of $346.19 million by 2005 (MOFA, 2006b)p.185. However, the truly innovative side to Japan's foreign policy regarding health is that it has shifted much of its support to NGOs and grass-roots groups for the implementation of its projects. Japan stresses the importance to operate through the UN and especially through the Trust Fund for Human Security. This fund was established by Japan in 1999 to support projects related to human security. Japan had provided almost $280 million to this fund by the end of 2006. The way in which this fund operates follows the human security framework in that the funds are channeled to other UN agencies which then in turn are given to local NGOs or grass-roots organizations for implementation. This includes the ownership and empowerment aspects of the paradigm.

An example of one such project is the assistance to "Support of Safe Motherhood in Nuba Mountains" Project in Sudan. Japan provided $1,298,374.21 to the United Nations Population Fund for this project. The project in discussion is significant in that it is part of the effort to consolidate peace in Sudan. The innovative approach of combining a health aspect with that of conflict resolution and peace consolidation is an integral part of the Human Security Paradigm. The project intended to tackle the high mortality rates in the area as well as supporting family planning. The project included strong elements of empowerment and participation such as the participation of the intended beneficiaries and consultation with the local community. The following are the activities included in the project: "provide **training** to 60 midwives and other service providers on family planning counseling and equipping family planning delivery points with contraceptives; **training** 200 midwives and 25 assistant health visitors at adequate professional institutions and to equip them with antenatal care and essential delivery services; **gaining community support** for midwifery service by holding workshops and distributing training materials; providing basic emergency obstetric care in adequately equipped facilities" (MOFA, 2006a). (emphasis added) The project shows a large content of capacity building and empowerment. This project sums up Japan's foreign policy regarding health and shows how different aspects of human security are treated as integral parts of a whole. This holistic approach can then be included in peace consolidation efforts such as the one in Sudan.

In conclusion, Japan has been actively promoting Human Security in the health field. The policies sponsored by Japan have tried to include health aspects in previously considered unrelated areas such as conflict resolution and peace consolidation. This is a field in which Japan can take a leadership role without worrying about its "historical guilt".

3.5 Japan's Policies Towards Grey Area Phenomena and Human Security

The end of the Cold War brought about a change in conflict. The nature of conflict shifted from one based on conventional warfare to less conventional forms such as terrorism, transnational crime, and ethnic strife just to mention a few. This led to the identification of the Grey Area Phenomena (GAP). GAP "can be loosely defined as threats to the stability of sovereign states by non-state actors and non-governmental processes and organizations" (William T. Tow, 2000). Peter A. Chalk divides GAP into two categories, namely violent GAP and non-violent GAP. Some examples of violent GAP are terrorism, crime syndicates, and drug trafficking while some representative examples of non-violent GAP are immigration, famine, and spread of diseases (William T. Tow, 2000). This section will concentrate on violent GAP and a human security approach to tackle them.

The first subtopic that will be discussed is transnational organized crime and illicit drugs. The Japanese government has taken several measures to combat money laundering such as supporting the Financial Task Force on Money Laundering (FATF) which is part of the Organization for Economic Cooperation and Development (MOFA, 2006b). In addition to that Japan is actively combating crime through the United Nations. This reflects Japan's declared UN-centered foreign policy (Dore, 1997). The Japanese government is currently in the process of passing national legislation in order to adopt the UN Convention against Transnational Organized Crime. Regarding illicit drugs, Japan was recently elected to the UN Commission on Narcotic Drugs and it introduced a draft which was passed as a resolution to promote cooperation in the field of abuse of legal drugs. This is an innovative approach to drug control since the abuse of legal substances has not usually been treated seriously at an international scale. Japan is also cooperating with the commission by providing expertise on the field of law enforcement regarding drug trafficking. Japan is not only combating illicit drugs at a macro level but has also donated $2.5 million to the United Nations Office on Drugs and Crime in the year 2005 (MOFA, 2006b). Most of the money donated was used in supporting projects related to law enforcement in Southeast Asia.

In order to understand Japan's holistic approach to drug trafficking it is necessary to look at a case study as an example of the overall human security strategy. The case in point is the "Support to ex-poppy farmers and poor vulnerable families in border areas" Project in Myanmar. This project began in January 29, 2007 and was funded by the UN Trust Fund for Human Security and by the Japanese Government. Due to the interdiciplinary nature of the project it was implemented by the "United Nations World Food Programme (WFP), the Food and Agriculture Organization of United Nations (FAO), the United Nations Office on Drugs and Crime (UNODC), and the United Nations Population Fund (UNFPA)" (MOFA, 2007). The total funding for the project was about $1 million and included activities aimed at promoting sustainable development. The project was intended to prevent, ameliorate, and protect the people from the ban on poppy production. The Shan state has relied heavily on this crop for its subsistence and thus its population has been affected by many threats to their human security. The first threat that should be mentioned is to their food security. The project has several activities geared at ameliorating the initial effects of the ban such as food-for-work plans, food-for-training plans, and food-for-education plans (MOFA, 2007). Therefore the first steps of the project are related to providing immediate aid in order to protect the people from food insecurity. This component is linked to the next which is to empower the people in order for them to get back on their feet. In other words, by including capacity building in the early stages of the project this will lead to other activities such as the introduction of alternative crops and improving the marketing and business abilities of the population. This in turn leads to sustainable development ergo food security. Nevertheless this is not the last component of the project, it includes a gender and health aspect. The overall project includes awareness-raising in the fields of gender and HIV/AIDS. This holistic approach is meant to provide overall human security to the target population in the Shan State. The project recognizes the need to go beyond simple humanitarian help and instead support and empower the people in order for them to achieve long lasting sustainable development and ultimately human security.

The previous example in addition to other more conventional approaches taken at the macro level point out to a succesful application of the Human Security framework in the field of transnational crime and illicit drugs by the Japanese government. The Human Security approach has helped in tackling these GAP problems at three levels simultaneously, at the global level through intergovernmental organizations (IGOs) and international regimes, at the national level through cooperation with national governments, and most importantly at the local level through community based projects which bring together international know-how in order to meet local needs.

3.6 Japan's Development Policy as a Predecessor of the Concept of Human Security

This section will cover arguments claiming that Japan's checkbook diplomacy combined with its historical internationalism give a result which is very similar to the concept of Human Security. According to this argument Japan's role has been far from reactive but rather has taken other forms of activity such as promoting international development and other forms of security. This argument centers on a basic question: Does Japan's adoption of the concept of Human Security reflect a shift in its foreign policy or just a continuation of its original foreign policy under a new name?

Japan has tried to pursue its foreign policy through economic means rather than by military means. This is evident in the promotion of economic development abroad. Japan has made use of official development assistance, foreign direct investment, and loans as a means of influencing other countries. This is a form of soft power in which the "iron triangle", the bureaucracy, big business, and the government, coordinate their policies in order to promote Japan's interests abroad. Nevertheless this policy of promoting development abroad did not involve many other factors other than economic considerations until the end of the cold war. There was a profound shift in this approach as the argument for and against the universality of human rights was at its height. With Asian leaders of countries such as Malaysia and Singapore promoting "Asian Values" rather than recognizing the universality of human rights, Japan was forced to take a stand in this controversial debate. Japan decided to side with the West and declared the universality of human rights and in addition to that followed the Western powers in deciding to promote democracy and free-market policies as parts of its development policy. Keizo Takemi reflects the Japanese point of view when saying that: "After the Cold War, the idea has become prominent within the advanced nations including Japan that human freedom, human rights, and democracy are universal values which serve as pillars around which the foundations for peace within the international community can be built" (Chen, 1995). Japan's approach towards this goals differed slightly from that of the other great powers in that it favored its promotion through economic rather than military means. In other words, Japan used the carrot more often than the stick. "Incorporating the argument for political conditionality that ties economic aid to democracy, Japan in 1992 made clear in one of the four principles of ODA that "along with the promotion of democratization in developing countries and efforts to introduce market-based economies, sufficient attention should be paid to the creation of conditions that secure basic human rights" (Chen, 1995). As Keizo Takemi explains, this marked a shift in Japanese policy. Its policy was still based on its economic power but started to include other parallel goals such as the promotion of human rights and democracy. This is important in that it included the possibility of intervention in the internal affairs of sovereign nations.

Another important factor behind Japan's foreign policy is its historical internationalism. Due to its experience in World War II as the only country to have suffered a nuclear attack, it has developed a sense of responsibility of helping the world avoid more such wars. This has engendered a feeling of internationalism that places much trust and emphasis on the United Nations and other intergovernmental organizations and on international development as a means to achieve greater security. This was based on the belief that by tackling the root causes of conflict global security could be achieved. This instrumental vision of development was quite revolutionary at the time especially coming from a state. In turn this reflects what Oliver Ramsbotham calls a "deep prevention" approach to conflict resolution (Oliver Ramsbotham, 2006). "Deep prevention aims to address the root causes, including underlying conflicts of interest and relationships. At the international level this may mean addressing recurrent issues and problems in the international system. Within societies, it may mean engaging with issues of *development*, political culture and community relations" (Oliver Ramsbotham, 2006). (emphasis added) This "deep prevention" approach to conflict resolution reflects many aspects of Human Security such as its emphasis on long term solutions and its stress on sustainability and what is especially significant about it is that it connects national well-being to global well-being. This is the missing link in most state's foreign policies and Japan realized this connection at a very early stage. Hook points out that: "The Japanese state and its people, then, harbor a view of security which is much broader than the military, or guns-bombs-and-tanks, approach found in most of the other major industrialized powers" (Glenn D. Hook, 2005). This broader view of security and a growing sense of internationalism in Japan can be observed in the comments made by ordinary Japanese people. It "was demonstrated by the reaction to the death of a young Japanese election monitor working as a UN volunteer in Cambodia. His father declared that in this son's memory he would devote himself to the cause of the UN and international solidarity. He wanted the world to know that there were people in Japan motivated "not by national interest, but by global citizenship, by the ideal of sharing global solidarity with the people of other countries." This led to 5,000 applications for the volunteer corps over the next two months" (Dore, 1997). Another example of this growing sense of internationalism can be observed in some of the proposed solutions to the debate over Japan's Peace Constitution and the limitation it imposes on its ability to participate in United Nations peacekeeping operations. Midori Yajima proposes the following: "And that leads to further reflection; if it were the case that members of the Self-Defense Forces who took part in peace-keeping activities were to suspend their Japanese citizenship in favor of UN citizenship, would there really be any need to amend the Japanese Constitution" (Dore, 1997)? As unlikely as this is to happen, it really shows that a large segment of the Japanese people are really thinking outside the box, they are thinking beyond the more traditional and atavistic forms of identity.

Now that we have looked at Japan's traditional checkbook diplomacy and its parallel internationalism we may go ahead to identify some trends. The two approaches are complementary. The first can be identified as an early form of comprehensive security with a heavy emphasis on "deep prevention" while the second provides that missing link between the local and the global. The internationalism which permeates that early form of comprehensive security makes the traditional Japanese approach very similar to the present day concept of Human Security. However, there is only one aspect that was still missing at that point and that is what is called "light prevention" in conflict resolution theory and what Human Security refers to as immediate threats. In addition to that another small but important ingredient was lacking. That was an emphasis on people rather than on the state. There was a shift from state centered international development to people centered development by the Japanese government during the late 1980s and especially during the 1990s. This shift will be discussed in more detail at a later section however it is important to note that the basic framework of the Human Security approach was already in place by the beginning of the 1990s. This in turn helps explain why it was so easy for Japan to accept Human Security as the pillar of its foreign policy. In addition to that this preexisting compatibility between the two approaches was further strengthened by an unlikely ally, the nationalists. This marriage of convenience was very important in allowing Japan to play a more important role in UN peace keeping operations and is slowly providing the most important missing instrumental ingredient, the ability to undertake "light prevention".

Table 2 Instrumental Human Security and its Objectives

Instrumental Security (means)	Security Objectives (ends)
Military	"freedom from fear" (survival/wellbeing)
Economic	"freedom from want" (survival/wellbeing)
Political	"freedom from fear" (survival/wellbeing)
Environmental	"freedom from fear"/ "freedom from want" (survival/wellbeing)

Note: Adapted from (Chen, 1995)

CHAPTER IV

JAPAN AND OFFICIAL DEVELOPMENT ASSISTANCE (ODA)

4.1 Brief Overview of the History of Japan's ODA Policy

Japan rejoined the international community in 1952 after the signing of the San Francisco Peace Treaty. At this time, Japan's most pressing foreign policy imperative was to re-establish peaceful diplomatic relations with most of the international community. In order to do that, Japan had to pay reparations for the damages caused by its war-time aggression. Some of the beneficiaries of that were countries such as Myanmar (Burma) and Indonesia, among others (Togo, 2005). Those reparations became the beginning of Japan's ODA policy. The estimated total of the reparations paid by Japan amounted to 945.53 billion yen, according to the Ministry of Foreign Affairs (Togo, 2005). Japan's ODA during the 1950s and most of the 1960s was characterized by its conditionality (MOFA, 2006c). This conditionality is not the one usually expected which includes respect for human rights and democracy but rather one that limited the way in which the aid could be used. Most of those reparations were paid with the transfer of outdated technology and industrial plants for example (Glenn D. Hook, 2005). The recipient had to use the aid to buy or pay for Japanese products or services. By doing this, Japan used its ODA to stimulate its economy and to increase the level of interdependency with the beneficiary (MOFA, 2006c). This policy went side by side with Japan's norm of "economism" and later on with its "GNPsm" both of which favored economic growth above all else. Some countries resented the conditionality of aid during this period with the argument that the money or loans provided could be more effectively used procuring local products and services or those of a third country.

The 1960s saw Japan's period of high speed growth and also a growing concern to find markets for its products. Thus ODA became an economic tool which served to open new markets and to find sources of raw materials. Regarding Japan's ODA policy during this period, it was very similar to that of the 1950s except that it became more conspicuous internationally due to Japan's rising importance, especially in East Asia. "Tied" aid was the norm during the 1960s and Japan started to realize that while it lacked military power, economic power could be just as useful and as powerful. In 1961 Japan was one of the founding members of the OECD's Development Assistance Committee (DAC) (Glenn D. Hook, 2005). Japan's ODA reached $100 million in 1964 and was mostly confined to Asia (Togo, 2005).

The 1970s were also characterized by large sized infrastructure projects and mostly "tied" aid. However changing trends in international development norms put some pressure on Japan to include other approaches as part of its ODA policy. One such approach was that of Basic Human Needs (BHN) (MOFA, 2006c). This approach stressed that aid should help satisfy the needs of the people, and benefit the recipient country as a whole, rather than only serve the economic agenda of the donor. This trend was contradicted by Japan's continuing policy of "tying" aid to Japanese products and services. In 1972 72 percent of aid was tied (Glenn D. Hook, 2005). In addition to that most of Japan's ODA was concentrated in the Asia-Pacific region. This decade saw ODA rise tenfold and it reached the staggering amount of $1.1 billion in 1976 (Togo, 2005).

The 1980s saw two important changes in Japan's ODA policy. The first was that structural adjustment and liberalization came to the fore (MOFA, 2006c). In addition to that Japan started to respond to negative criticism by developing countries over its policy of "tying" aid to Japanese products and services by "untying" all aid by 1982 (Glenn D. Hook, 2005). Nevertheless Japanese Official Development Aid continued to be "tied" in practice. This is due to the practice of granting aid through private companies operating in the beneficiary countries. In other words this means that the common practice was for the government to present a request with the help and guidance of a Japanese company. This means that the petitioning company will usually provide the products or the services. According to Glenn Hook this helped Japanese transnational corporations penetrate foreign markets and thus increased interdependency and trade (Glenn D. Hook, 2005).

The end of the Cold War and continued economic success meant that Japan increased its ODA during the early 1990s (MOFA, 2006c). In 1991 Japan became the number one donor in the world and held that position until the onset of the 1997 Asian economic crisis. Before the economic crisis Japan made great efforts to promote its peculiar style of development based on strong government guidance over the private sector and trade. Those feelings of success were voiced in the much discussed 1993 World Bank report entitled "The East Asian Miracle" (MOFA, 2006c). This report represented the apex of Asian pride and also served as a summary of what Japan and its East Asian followers believed was the key to successful development. It favored the "developmental state model" and was also implicitly used by Japan to justify its "flying geese model" and the division of labor it had created in Asia. In summary it declared that Japan had a great influence through its ODA and other economic policies in the development of East Asia. From a more qualitative point of view Japan's ODA underwent major changes during this decade. The end of the Cold War drastically changed world order and Japan was awakened to that fact by the Gulf War.

After this event, Japan realized that more aid should be allocated for peacebuilding, peacemaking, peacekeeping, and finally for the protection of those affected by conflict. Conflict prevention was also emphasized and by the end of the decade and the beginning of the 21st century, the trend was moving towards nation building and a more comprehensive development approach.

The late 1980s through the early 21st century saw another interesting change in Japan's ODA policy. This is related to human rights and democracy. While always claiming to promote the concepts of human rights and democracy, Japan was known for its staunch opposition to connecting economics to those more political issues. In other words, Japan was historically keen to separate human rights and democracy from economic considerations. This started to change slightly in the late 1980s initially due to Western Pressure and the growing polarization over the issue of the universality of human rights. Most of East Asia upheld that Asian values were superior and had precedence over human rights. Japan was then forced to take a stand on this issue, at least officially, that supported the position of the Western Powers which claimed that human rights are universal. It can not be denied that this was mostly done due to Western pressure like in the case of the Tiananmen massacre when Japan temporarily stopped ODA to China. However Japan did try to persuade its Western allies to resume it as soon as possible. According to Aoi and others, this trend increased steadily as can be seen in the 1992 ODA Charter which includes some conditions to qualify for ODA (Aoi, 2000). Finally during the late 1990s and the early 21st century global conditions such as the rise of virulent nationalism and terrorism forced Japan to reconsider its historic apathy towards using ODA as a tool to promote the respect of human rights and the spread of democracy (Togo, 2005). The reasons for this shift are complex and involve many actors. But one important factor is the tightening of the security alliance with the United States and also a growing understanding of the connections between development and security. The climax of this came about with the development of the concept of human security. This concept was eagerly adopted by Japan so as to bring some coherence to its foreign policy. While the concept effectively incorporates most aspects of Japan's foreign policy, the question is whether it served as an actually different and innovative approach to guide Japan's foreign policy towards a single direction or rather just served as a way to justify incoherent policy goals formulated through complex political interactions which in reality serve to hide other very different policy goals. In other words, the following sections will trace back the history of the concept in relation to Japan's ODA policy and then draw from that Japan's official position regarding the term. In addition to that, Japan's official position regarding the term will be analyzed and tested in order to find inconsistencies and contradictions that may provide some useful insights for the more comprehensive case study analysis that will be provided in the following chapter.

4.1.1 Brief Quantitative Overview of Japan's ODA

The present section will provide a brief overview of Japan's ODA policy based on quantitative considerations. While the author considers that quantitative data is insufficient for a holistic interpretation of Japan's ODA policy, its inclusion is helpful to show the validity of this assertion. One recent study dealing with Japan's ODA policy towards Southeast Asia is based almost entirely on quantitative analysis, namely that by Trinidad (Trinidad, 2007). The following paragraph will interpret some of the quantitative data available on Japan's ODA and mention some of the

conclusions reached by Trinidad's interpretations.

Table 3 Regional Distribution of Japanese Bilateral ODA (in US$ million)

Region	1985	1990	1995	1998	2000	2002	2004
Total	2557	6941	10557.06	8606.90	9640.10	6725.91	5954.10
Asia	1732	4117	5745.34	5372.03	5283.82	4085.56	2544.56
ASEAN	(46%)	(56%)	(39%)	(44%)	(59%)	(43%)	(35%)
	800	2299	2229	2356	3126	1748	897.04
Middle East	201	705	721	392	727	209	1030.87
Africa	252	792	1333	950	969	585	646.97
Latin America	225	561	1142	553	800	592	309.30
Oceania	24	114	160	147	151	94	42.15
Europe	1	158	153	144	118	121	140.69
Unspecified	122	494	1303	1048	1592	1043	1239.56

Note: Adapted from (Trinidad, 2007, p. 107). "Total may not add up due to rounding. The percentage in the parentheses pertains to the share of ASEAN in the ODA disbursements to Asia (Trinidad, 2007, p. 107)".

Let us first look at Japan's ODA divided by region. Table 3 shows the regional

distribution of Japanese bilateral ODA. It is clear that Asia historically has always

received the largest share of ODA. In 2004 Asia's share was 2544.56 million dollars

from a total of 5954.10 million dollars. Now let us look at ASEAN's share.

Percentages show that while ASEAN's share remains the larger than any other region,

it has decreased proportionally in recent years. Trinidad provides a few interesting

reasons for this shift. The emphasis placed on helping Africa by the Millennium

Development Goals and Japan's increasing interest in participating in nation-building

and peace-making in the Middle East. This explains the obvious increase in aid to the

Middle East and the decline in proportional aid to ASEAN.

From table 3 is it also clear that Japan's ODA has steadily declined from its

maximum level in 1995 to the present. The gap between the previously mentioned maximum level of 10557.06 million dollars and 2004's level of 5954.10 is quite considerable. The reasons of this are clearly linked to the 1997 Asian Financial Crisis and the continued difficulties encountered by the Japanese economy. Due to this Japanese ODA Policy has had to operate under strict budget constraints and has had to make more strategic use of its ODA. Trinidad states that the budget constraints under which Japan is operating reflects domestic pressure to make more strategic use of ODA as an "earning" strategy while Japan's increased ODA to the Middle East and Africa shows international pressure favoring a "spending" strategy. While Trinidad's observations are useful in order to help understand some of the pressures under which Japanese policy makers operate it is also overly simplistic to divide ODA policy between "spending" and "earning" strategies (Trinidad, 2007). This is one clear drawback of basing a full interpretation of Japan's ODA on quantitative data. It is impossible to know the true intentions behind Japan's allocation of ODA by just looking at cold numbers. Nevertheless a close look at Table 3 will provide the reader with necessary data in order to understand the context under which Japanese policy makers are operating.

A look at quantitative data related to the actual make-up of ODA to ASEAN countries provides mixed results. As shown in Table 4, Japanese ODA is composed basically of grant aid and loans. Ten member countries of ASEAN are shown and the ODA they received from 1994 to 2004 has been divided into grant aid and loans. It is clear that Indonesia, the Philippines, and Thailand have been the major recipients and that Vietnam is another country received increasing amounts of Japanese ODA. Also aid to the relatively developed economies of Thailand and Indonesia has been mostly composed of loans while aid provided to the less developed members of ASEAN such as Cambodia and Laos has been mostly composed of grant aid. This could have something to do with ability to repay loans and most importantly with Japan's view about the strength of the economy in question. A good point made by Trinidad is Japan's increasing aid to Vietnam. As can be seen in Table 4 most aid to Vietnam has been in the form of loans which shows that Japan believes in Vietnams economic future and in the growing strength of its economy.

Table 4 Japan's ODA to ASEAN by Type of aid (in US$ million)

ASEAN 10	ODA 1991-2004		
	ODA	Loan	Grant
Brunei	(10) 24.91	0	24.91
Cambodia	(5) 952.69	12.53	940.16
Indonesia	(1) 11296.32	8517.19	2779.04
Laos	(6) 950.34	14.02	936.33
Malaysia	(8) 312.96	-551.72	864.64
Myanmar	(7) 765.37	-59.36	830.74
Philippines	(2) 5831.77	3504.26	2327.50
Singapore	(9) 99.46	-3.66	103.12
Thailand	(3) 5802.83	4086.66	1716.16
Vietnam	(4) 4344.67	3073.88	1270.80

Note: Adapted from (Trinidad, 2007, p. 112) Grant includes technical assistance. Loan is total disbursement less payment. Numbers in parenthesis are ranks.

A quantitative analysis of Japan's ODA reveals a few interesting trends. Japan's ODA has decreased since the onset of the 1997 Asian Financial Crisis. Japan considers Asia to be of great importance and thus had provided most of its ODA to this region. Nevertheless, recent events have prompted Japan to divert some of its ODA to other regions such as Africa and the Middle East. Japan's ODA to ASEAN has always being considerable. ODA to the more advanced economies of Southeast Asia tends to be composed mostly of loans while that to the less advanced ones tends to be mostly in the form of grants. Finally, Vietnam is receiving increasingly large amounts of aid in the form of loans.

The following sections will deal with the actual topic of the present dissertation which is a discursive analysis of Japan's ODA policy regarding the concept of Human Security.

4.2 Human Security and Japan's Official ODA Policy

4.2.1 Overview of Early Discourse

Japan adopted the concept of human security as an important part of its foreign policy as early as 1998 but it took a while longer for it to permeate more specific areas such as ODA policy. This is evident in the 1999 Diplomatic Bluebook in which an entire subsection of chapter 2 was devoted to human security in general under the more general topic of the betterment of global society (MOFA, 1999b). This overview of the concept was intended as a general introduction and as an attempt to bring some cohesion to Japan's foreign policy in general. A more specific application of the concept of human security can be found in connection to Japan's policy towards developing countries and Official Development Assistance. Section 3 includes a few paragraphs on the importance of the concept for a better understanding of the problems caused by the 1997 economic crisis and how Japan interprets the concept in relation to its ODA. It is worthy of quoting two important passages that summarize Japan's official position. "Human security comprehensively covers all the menaces that threaten human survival, daily life and dignity-for example, environmental degradation, violations of human rights, transnational organized crime, illicit drugs, refugees, poverty, antipersonnel landmines, and other infectious diseases such as AIDS-and strengthens efforts to confront these threats." The explanation then continues by saying that "As these are all cross-border issues, coordinated action by the international community will be important, as will linkages and cooperation among governments, international organizations, NGOs and other parts of civil society" (MOFA, 1999a). The first excerpt provides a general definition of the concept. It is important to note the general and loose nature of the definition provided. This definition is then complemented by the second quote which gives a glimpse at the concept in practice, the approach. In summary Human Security is defined as including all the threats that affect a person's quality of life and also recognizes that those threats concern actors at all levels, from the individual, to the global level. It is evident that this view of Human Security is as broad as can be and that therefore the commitment it implies is so great that at the end it is very little. In other words, this initial introduction of the concept of Human Security by the Japanese government is very broad and simply tries to include almost everything covered by its previous ODA policy by a simple umbrella-term, human security. In addition to that, the short mention it includes about the actual approach or methodology simply recommends that a concerted action is needed in order to tackle a long list of threats. Thus the first time the concept of Human Security is mentioned in Japanese ODA policy is superficial.

Another important official document about ODA policy published in the same year is the yearly ODA Country Policy towards major recipients (MOFA, 1999c).

This document does not mention the concept of human security and while including some approaches which are potentially compatible with this approach, a large portion of it deals with macroeconomic considerations and a traditional top-down approach. This division is present in all of the country policies included but the section on the Philippines will serve as a representative example. This section is divided into two parts. The first part deals with contemporary development trends such as sustainable development and human development while the second represents a modern day example of structural adjustment policies and modernization theory. So as to convince the reader of the validity of the previous assertions let us analyze a representative excerpt from the first section of this document. This section identified four key points that guide Japan's ODA policy towards the Philippines which are: sustainable growth, "mitigation of disparities", "environmental conservation and disaster management", and "human resources development and institution building" (MOFA, 1999c). This part represents the softer side of development and while it remains top-down it does give some consideration to environmental and humanitarian concerns.

The second part of the Country Policy for the Philippines moves even closer to a complete top-down approach based on neo-liberal structural adjustment. This is evident in the following excerpt. "Structural reform of the economy must be pursued through measures such as stabilizing budget expenditure and revenue, improving the current balance, resolving the problem of cumulative debts and deregulation; the promotion of trade investment and improving of the banking system must also be pursued" (MOFA, 1999c). The rest of the section is very similar in nature to the previous excerpt and thus it is clear that the second part of Japan's country policy on ODA for the Philippines does not reflect the concept of Human Security and instead more closely resembles World Bank recommendations and traditional neo-liberal economic prescriptions.

In summary, the concept of Human Security first appeared in Japan's diplomatic Bluebook in 1999. At this point it was introduced by means of a short overview of the concept in the general introduction of the book and also by means of a brief introductory section in the chapter dealing with Developing countries and ODA. The concept of Human Security did not permeate more deeply into more specific sections of the Bluebook and while the chapters dealing with ODA such as Chapter 2 has an introductory subsection about the concept, the rest of the chapter does not mention the concept again and does not show any signs of any kind of influence the concept may have had on actual policies. Another clear example of this lack of cohesion, at this point in time, was shown to be found in Japan's ODA policy towards major recipients. The document in discussion does not mention the concept of human security and while including some compatible practices such as environmental conservation and environmental protection, it does not apply the human security approach and instead follows the standard top-down approach.

The 2000 Diplomatic Bluebook is a good example of how the concept of Human Security rose in importance in a single year. The 2000 edition includes Human Security as one the pillars of Japanese foreign policy. It is also significant that the concept is mentioned in the first page of the entire Diplomatic Bluebook. The introduction of the overview begins by explaining the importance of individual-focused measures and of protecting human dignity. The document then continues to stress the importance of non-profit organizations in dealing with threats to individuals. Finally the first page of the overview mentions the concept of Human Security and

Japan's economic support for the establishment of the Trust Fund for Human Security as part of the United Nations (MOFA, 2000b).

Chapter two of the 2000 Diplomatic Bluebook deals specifically with Human Security. This overview begins with a very general definition of Human Security: "Japan emphasizes "Human Security" from the perspective of strengthening efforts to cope with threats to human lives, livelihoods and dignity as poverty, environmental degradation, illicit drugs, transnational organized crime, infectious diseases such as HIV/AIDS, the outflow of refugees and anti-personnel land mines..." (MOFA, 2000a) The document then traces the history of Japan's support for the concept such as when former Primer Minister Obuchi first mentioned the concept in 1998 in a Conference entitled "An Intellectual Dialogue on Building Asia's Tomorrow" in which he declared that he wanted the 21st century to be human-centered (MOFA, 2000a). The Prime Minister then mentioned the concept again in Hanoi and in a meeting with the representatives of the Nordic countries in 1999. The concept was first officially connected to development in 1999 in a Conference jointly organized by the United Nations University and the Ministry of Foreign Affairs. This shows that Japan was making an attempt to mainstream the concept of Human Security in order for the international community to accept it. This strategy was by no means hidden or undercover but on the contrary Japan explicitly declared it to be its intention. "As observed above, Japan is leading discussion on "Human Security" in the international community, while undertaking the implementation of concrete policies. These efforts will be strengthened in the years to come, positioning "Human Security" as a key perspective in developing Japan's foreign policy" (MOFA, 2000a). The previous excerpt from the 2000 Diplomatic Bluebook summarizes Japan's strategy regarding the mainstreaming of Human Security while remaining vague regarding the true intentions behind this intended paradigmatic shift or discursive co-optation.

In summary official policy discourse regarding human security during the late 1990s and the early 21st century, increasingly give importance to the concept of Human Security. While the concept rapidly occupied center-stage as Japan's basic doctrine regarding its foreign policy, it did not manage to permeate all areas of it. In other words, as shown in the 1999 Diplomatic Bluebook diffusion of the concept moved from the overview to other more specific areas of foreign policy.

4.2.2   The 2003 Official Development Assistance Charter and Human Security

Next, we will look at the most important document regarding Japan's ODA policy, the 2003 Official Development Assistance Charter. This document begins by clearly stating the general goals behind Japan's Official Development. This is succinctly put by stating that "the Objectives of Japan's ODA are to contribute to the peace and development of the international community, and thereby to help ensure Japan's own security and prosperity" (MOFA, 2003). It should be noted that the previously mentioned goal is perfectly compatible with human security and recognizes the global interdependence emphasized by the concept of Human Security. The document then proceeds to explain Japan's basic policies regarding ODA. It is notable that those policies reflect the concept of Human Security. For example the first stresses the importance of self-help efforts and ownership. In addition to that it also mentions the importance of promoting democracy and human rights in conjunction with development efforts (MOFA, 2003). The second policy deals with the perspective of "human security" and mainly concentrates on the concept's emphasis on human dignity and its perspective on threats on individuals. The Document clearly states that Japan will provide assistance to protect human dignity and for the empowerment of individuals (MOFA, 2003). In other words, the document made an explicit promise to apply the concept of Human Security in the implementation of its ODA. "Accordingly, Japan will implement ODA to strengthen the capacity of local communities through human resource development. To ensure that human dignity is maintained at all stages, from the conflict stage to the reconstruction and development stages, Japan will extend assistance for the protection and empowerment of individuals" (MOFA, 2003). The third basic policy complements the previous ones by emphasizing the importance of taking care of the most vulnerable first, a statement that echoes the ethos of Human Security (MOFA, 2003). The fourth deals with Japan sharing its development experience and expertise while the fifth and final policy stresses collaboration. The document links the first four policies by stressing the importance of collaboration and partnership with all members of the international community. It states that in order for ODA to make a difference it has to be planned and implemented in collaboration with NGOs, private companies, intergovernmental organizations, and international financial institutions (MOFA, 2003). It is evident that the previously mentioned basic policies regarding Japan's ODA policy embody the concept of Human Security not only as an idea but also as an approach.

Four Priority Issues are mentioned: poverty reduction (including environmental and health aspects), sustainable growth (intellectual property rights, and macroeconomic growth), global issues (development of international norms), and peace-building (comprehensive assistance for nation-building) (MOFA, 2003). While maintaining the same tone as the section on basic policies, the section on priority issues is more traditional in nature and deals with issues such as macroeconomic growth and intellectual rights that do not necessarily stress the concept of Human Security. Nevertheless it is important to recognize that those traditional foreign policy concerns such as peace-building and economic growth have been influenced by the Human Security approach specially when dealing with their implementation. For example, rather than promoting economic growth as an end, the document recognizes some of the dangers of unsustainable economic growth and also the connections it may have to health and environmental considerations. The same holds true in the case of peace-building and conflict prevention for which a comprehensive approach is recommended and also one that protects the most vulnerable while promoting long term development.

The 2003 ODA Charter states that East Asia is a priority region due to geographic proximity and the level of economic and cultural interconnectedness it has with Japan. ASEAN is mentioned as of significance importance for Japan. This region maintained high rates of economic growth during the 1990s and is a very important market of Japanese good and services, in addition to that it is also an importance source of raw materials and labor for Japan and its transnational corporations (TNCs). As a result of this interconnectedness Japan maintains that its focus on this region for purposes of ODA is justified and necessary. While clearly showing economic considerations as an important motive behind Japan's prioritization of this region, there is also an aspect of Human Security in that the Charter includes the important goals of reducing disparities in this region and of promoting economic partnerships as a more human security-friendly way of promoting economic growth and trade (MOFA, 2003).

Japan's principles of ODA implementation tend to be controversial due to the conditionality they entail. While the ideals they embody are almost universally accepted, some NGOs and developing countries tend to view them as unacceptable intervention in their internal affairs. In order to understand why this is so we will review the four principles of ODA implementation. The first deals with environmental conservation. This means that theoretically Japan will give priority to projects or beneficiaries who promote environmental conservation and thus sustainable development. This clearly reflects Human Security in that environmental threats can be important sources of insecurity for vulnerable populations. The second principle deals with the actual use of ODA funds. It clearly states that it should not be used under any circumstances for military purposes. This also reflects the human security approach which stresses non-military solutions to international problems. The third principle also deals with the military but does not only include the use of ODA funds but even looks at the way in which a certain country spends money on the military or on weapons of mass destruction. Conditionality is probably one of the most controversial principles since it states that Japan may refuse ODA on the grounds of undue military expenditures or for the illegal possession or production of weapons of mass destruction. While it is evident that Japan has historically overlooked clear violations of the previously mentioned principles it is important that they are stated so that Japan reserves the right to refuse ODA at any time for internal reasons. The previous statement clearly reflects the concept of Human Security and not only the watered down UNDP version but also the more comprehensive approach espoused by

Middle Powers such as Canada and Australia, also known as protective Human Security. The fourth and final principle is also the most comprehensive and arguably controversial of all of them, and states the following: "Full attention should be paid to efforts for promoting democratization and the introduction of a market-oriented economy, and the situation regarding the protection of basic human rights and freedoms in the recipient country" (MOFA, 2003). The fourth and last principle includes important aspects of Human Security such as the promotion of democratization which implicitly includes empowerment and participation and the protection of human rights. It is also interesting to note that Japan includes the introduction of a market-oriented economy in the same category as basic human rights and democracy. While democracy and human rights are part of human security a market-oriented economy does not necessarily lead to human security and thus should not be grouped with the others. The four principles represent a strong version of human security which goes beyond ideals and set up, at least potentially, practical measures that can be used in order to use ODA as a weapon or tool in order to promote Human Security strategically. In other words, the concept of conditionality in this case recognizes the interconnectedness of all threats and also makes the much needed assertion that some threats are internal and are caused by faulty national policies and blatant human rights violations caused by a diverse array of factors such as selfish military dictatorships or atavistic traditional local practices. In this respect Japan's approach to human security regarding ODA goes beyond a human needs approach, and sustainable development by recognizing the legitimate needs of potential beneficiaries and their right to ownership while also understanding that some external guidance is necessary in order to tackle local conditions that cause insecurity and thus make better use of ODA.

Finally the document stresses the need for collaboration with aid-related entities such as Japanese NGOs, and also local NGOs in order to more effectively implement ODA projects. It is important to note that the charter does not make the frequent mistake of omitting the private sector as a valuable partner and instead stresses the importance of collaborating with the private sector both from Japan and local in order to their technologies and expertise (MOFA, 2003). The charter also mentions other important stakeholders such a local governments, universities and economic organizations. This constructive approach taken by Japan contrasts with that taken by more radical non-governmental organizations (NGOs) which demonize the private sector together with economic organizations and thus ignore valuable sources of funds and expertise. It should be remembered that Human Security is a holistic approach that stresses the importance of a comprehensive approach to solving and ameliorating human insecurity. This implies that in order to tackle such as vast array of threats ranging from environmental ones to health-related ones more is needed that simply talking to the village elder or the most prominent shaman of the tribe. While important too, the elder and the shaman are not sufficient to tackle such daunting problems and thus Japan's official approach to the implementation of ODA is more in tune with the concept of Human Security than other contemporary competitors in the field of international development.

4.2.3 Recent ODA Policy Developments and Human Security

The present section will cover developments in official ODA policy from 2004 to the present and will try to show how the concept of human security has been increasingly reflected in them. One relatively early example of this batch of official documents is a statement of the Ministry of Foreign Affairs regarding ODA and NGOs. The 2004 Statement on Partnerships with NGOs for the purpose of ODA is a brief attempt by the government at explaining how it was striving to solve one of its greatest weaknesses (MOFA, 2004). Japan is an interesting case in that its civil society is relatively weak considering its economic power and level of development. There are around 400 Japanese NGOs which according to the Ministry of Foreign Affairs lag behind their European and American counterparts in organization and human resources (MOFA, 2004). Nevertheless the Japanese government recognizes that this is an important area that needs attention and that in order to fully adopt the human security approach to development it must strengthen and cooperate with both Japanese and local NGOs. The document in question states three main principles in order to have a good partnership with NGOs: dialogue, collaboration, and support (MOFA, 2004). Dialogue refers to the exchange of information and views at all stages of the policy making process so as to include the point of view of NGOs and their experience at the grassroots level in ODA policy. Collaboration mostly refers to sharing responsibility in implementation of ODA funded projects and also exchanges of human resources and expertise. While the third principle, support, is mostly one sided and reflects the Ministry of Foreign Affairs' commitment to support the development of Japanese NGOs by funding them and also by providing them with necessary expertise. It should be noted at this point that the three principles reflect the concept of human security and of the most recent development studies trends. Input is requested at all stages of the process and implementation is also delegated to those in direct contact with the grassroots beneficiaries. This means that this approach is both holistic and participatory in nature. Therefore while this document does not explicitly mention the concept of Human Security it does reflect important elements of it and more broadly is perfectly compatible with its approach to development.

It is important to look at the concrete measures taken to put into practice the previously explained principles. The first measure is that of the Japan Platform which was established in 2000 as a way to facilitate the cooperation of the government, the private sector, and NGOs for humanitarian relief (MOFA, 2004). The previous measure is certainly not the earliest one but it is the most holistic and ambitious in nature. The three sectors are brought together in order to cooperate for a single goal which in this case is humanitarian relief. This Platform tries to promote the seamless integration of the three main sectors of Japanese society in order to maximize the combined resources and expertise for Japan's humanitarian relief projects. The way in which this platform actually works is through a combination of formal and informal consultations and a loose network of Japanese companies and NGOs both at home and abroad. Their activities are coordinated by Japanese official representatives dispatched around the world in diplomatic missions and at home more directly with the Ministry itself.

A third measure taken in order to facilitate cooperation with NGOs for purposes of ODA planning and implementation is older than the previously explained one but is more limited in nature. The NGO Subsidy and the Grant Assistance for Grassroots Projects date back to 1989 and represent a one way exchange of resources from the government to NGOs. While limited in scope, this measure does have some beneficial effects such as strengthening NGOs and transferring some of the responsibility of implementations to the civil sector. In other words, by channeling

ODA through NGOs the resulting projects will arguably be more participatory in nature and closer to the actual beneficiaries. In addition to that, the funds channeled through the Grant Assistance for Grassroots Projects will be more likely to have an effect on individual human security than macro projects channeled through large aid organizations or national governments. It should be noted that this measure is not limited to Japanese NGOs and therefore includes local NGOs which are more likely to know the actual needs and threats related to a certain community.

The third measure to be discussed is limited to Japanese NGOs and consists mostly of Grant Assistance for Japanese NGO projects and the Japan International Cooperation Agency's (JICA) Partnership Program (MOFA, 2004). The main goal of this measure is to foster the strength of Japanese NGOs as a useful tool for ODA. By limiting the target organizations to those of Japanese origin the Ministry of Foreign Affairs expects Japanese NGOs to be strengthened and for them to eventually develop to the level of their European and American counterparts.

In summary the Statement by the Ministry of Foreign Affairs on the Partnership with Japanese NGOs under ODA does not mention the concept of Human Security while it does reflect the approach.

The first document to make comprehensive use of the Human Security approach is the latest Medium-Term Policy on Official Development Assistance which was passed on February 4, 2005 (MOFA, 2005). This document is one of the three most important documents on ODA policy following the ODA Charter. It represents the direction policy will take for five years while the ODA Charter has a longer term in nature and the Individual Country Policies are more narrow in nature.

Due to the length and importance of this document the next few pages will be devoted to the careful description, explanation, and analysis of it.

The Medium-Term Policy on ODA deals with six main issues: human security, poverty reduction, sustainable growth, global issues, peace-building, and measures for better implementation. The first is described as a central perspective of the Charter, the next four are priority issues, and the last deals with effectiveness. It is important to note at this point that Japan's stance on ODA according to the introduction of the Midterm Policy is to promote its strategic and effective use. This reflects a decrease in the total size of Japanese ODA starting with the 1997 financial crisis. In addition to that while the document in discussion treats human security as a separate area of interest, it is evident throughout the paper that it permeates its entirety.

The first major section of the document deals with the concept of human security and attempts to connect the concept to the present state of affairs, in other words to global issues such as the uncertainties caused by increasing globalization, terrorism, *inter alia*, and the effects they have on the most vulnerable. The definition provided of Human Security does not shine for its originality and remains as broad and vague as the one provided by the ODA Charter however it is more concise and does a good job at linking the concept to the approach. In other words, this definition stresses the fact that Human Security is not only a concept but more importantly it is an approach to development. "'Human Security' means focusing on individual people and building societies in which everyone can live with dignity by protecting and empowering individuals and communities that are exposed to actual or potential threats" (MOFA, 2005). This document is also the first instance in which the informal definition of human security as "freedom from want" and "freedom from fear" is used.

The most notable characteristic of this policy paper is that it includes a section on actual approaches on assistance necessary in order to achieve "human security". The Midterm Policy Paper on ODA clearly links them to the four policy issues identified in the introduction. The first point states that ODA should be made up of "assistance that puts people at the center of concerns and that effectively reaches the people" (MOFA, 2005). This point clearly states that ODA should be people-centered, which is the principal postulate of Human Security. The next two points are linked to empowerment and ownership: "assistance to strengthen local communities" and "assistance that emphasizes empowering of people" and that views them as "promoters of development" and aims to make them self-reliant (MOFA, 2005). The fourth point deals with assistance to those who are most vulnerable to threats and also briefly discusses how those threats should be tackled in a comprehensive way thus including not only "freedom from fear" but also "freedom from want". This is important in that due to the already discussed limitations faced by Japan's foreign policy, economic factors embodied by "freedom from want" are given equal importance to more traditional concerns of security such as "freedom from fear". The fifth point is probably the most controversial and contradictory one. This one is deals with respect for cultural diversity and how ODA should respect it. It states that cultural diversity should be protected while at the same time the individual should be protected so that their human rights are not violated in the name of culture (MOFA, 2005). The ambiguity here is evident since it is very difficult to know where to draw the line between cultural practices and violations to human rights. Nevertheless this simply reflects the same ambiguity expressed by the UN Commission on Human Security and other supporters of the development view of Human Security, and therefore arguably they are just following the trend. However, this point can be contentious due to Japan's support for the universality of human rights and due to its collaboration with the western democracies in nation-building in the Middle East. In other words, it should be noted that this presents and example of incongruity and a gap between discourse and implementation.

The final point deals with implementation and more specifically with Human Security's emphasis on a holistic approach. It stresses the need for what it calls "cross-sectoral assistance" that involves a vast array of actors and pools their expertise in order to achieve human security (MOFA, 2005). This point is also notable in that it explicitly stresses the need for professional expertise in order to tackle structural problems. This is a point in which the Japanese approach to human security slightly diverges from the one held by most grass root organizations and some NGOs. While the second stresses the importance of community based development and empowerment and usually disregard and at times even demonize professional expertise and structural adjustments, the former is mindful of the complementary nature of the two approaches.

The following sections of the Midterm Policy on ODA are the most interesting one from the point of view of Human Security permeation into other policy areas. While they deal with the four priority issues and peace-building it is important to note that the term "human security" is mentioned a plurality of times and that every effort is made to bring cohesion to the different sections through the use of the human security approach as policy glue. The transition between the previously explained section dealing specifically with the human security approach to assistance to the section on the four priority issues of poverty reduction, sustainable growth, addressing global issues, and peace-building is made through the use of basic principles reflecting human security which are applied to the specific issues. Those basic principles are: promoting ownership through self-help efforts of developing countries, adoption of the "human security" perspective, equity, utilization of Japan's experience and expertise, and finally concerted action with the international community as well as fostering South to South cooperation (MOFA, 2005). This may seem repetitive considering that most of the principles are already included in the previous section's approaches to official development aid, nevertheless their reiteration serves to bring cohesion to the paper and most importantly to enhance policy coherence. Furthermore, the use of the term human security as a bridge between these two sections is both a sign of the importance of the term in ODA policy discourse and of the ambiguity and vagueness of its nature. However at this point the most important thing is to note the use of the term, and its centrality in ODA discourse as exemplified by the Midterm Policy on ODA.

The level of permeation will become increasingly clear as the four priority issues are analyzed. The first issue to be discussed is that of poverty reduction. This is an important point due to its close connection to vulnerability and "freedom from want". The paper treats this topic with caution and chooses to begin with poverty reduction and protection for the vulnerable instead of with growth and macroeconomic stabilization. The document makes a few important points on the general nature of poverty reduction. It mentions the Millennium Development Goals (MDGs) and the complex nature of poverty which involves economic as well as social aspects. Then it goes on to link that to East Asia's experience with development and emphasizes the obvious correlation between poverty reduction and economic growth.

Finally it moves on to reiterate its commitment to local development efforts and implies that the complexity of poverty requires locally planned development (MOFA, 2005).

Let us analyze the previously described passage. While stressing the importance of local development efforts and of social as well as economic aspects of poverty, the document also includes the example of East Asian development as an instance in which economic growth was observed to help reduce poverty. The important thing here is that while clearly alluding to the importance of free trade and structural adjustment, the document embellishes the message by embedding it in the larger concept of human security. This is a clear example of discourse formation in which the language of human security is used as a vehicle to promote free market policies. This will become clearer as the specific policies for poverty reduction are described.

The first approach prescribes "cross-sectoral assistance that is tailored to the stages of development" (MOFA, 2005) of a country. This point includes such things as cooperation with NGOs and local communities so as to determine their needs and also the aspect of prevention. It is clear that this approach echoes that of human security and is simply a repetition of already mentioned ideas to the problem of poverty reduction. Therefore it can be seen that Official Discourse is making an attempt at justifying all policy areas through the perspective of human security. Thus this is another instance of discourse permeation by Human Security. The next approach directly follows the previous one and as expected deals with direct assistance to the poor (MOFA, 2005). This point stresses the need for empowerment and ownership. It also includes the need for safety in order to protect the most vulnerable from sudden downturns and disasters. The previous point is again a direct application of the concept of human security to the problem of poverty reduction. However the next point is even more interesting due to its macroeconomic nature. It deals with the use of economic growth for poverty reduction. While dealing with a very old topic of traditional development the way in which it is treated is relatively innovative. It stresses the importance to promote economic growth while keeping in mind that equity must be promoted and that that equity should not only be that between individuals but also between rural and urban areas and between sectors such as agriculture and industry. The passage also recommends job creation as a possible measure to be taken and the promotion of labor-intensive enterprises and micro-finance. To the careful eye the mention of direct foreign investment (FDI) is notable. The passage in discussion includes two important elements of traditional economic growth, the promotion of tourism, and of foreign direct investment. While the passage does not dwell on those two topics and only mentions them on very positive terms and only in passing, they are concealed in a myriad of other development concerns such as safety nets, and ownership and camouflashed with the language of human security.

The next approach to poverty reduction deals with assistance to institutions and policies to reduce poverty. This is a blatant example of traditional development and a hint of concealed modernization theory in Japan's ODA policy. "In order to reduce poverty, it is important to establish institutions and policies that protect the rights of the poor based on the principle of equality under the law, and to enable the poor to participate in political activities and to exercise their capabilities. Assistance will therefore be provided to contribute to the protection of human rights, the rule of law, and the promotion of democratization"(MOFA, 2005). The previous excerpt from the Midterm Policy on ODA dealing with poverty reduction is apparently innocuous however a closer look will reveal the hidden message behind the language of human security. It should be obvious that the previous passage is highly intrusive and explicitly states that ODA will be used in order to promote institutions and policies which promote democracy, human rights, and the rule of law. The problem here, is how to interpret those concepts. Democracy is very problematic in that respect for while most developing countries in Asia interpret it as greater participation and equity at the local level, Japan and most of the Western Democracies interpret it as having elections and democratic accountability. Another term that is potentially problematic is human rights for while most Eastern developing countries emphasize economic and cultural rights, Japan and the Western Democracies favor political and civil rights. Final the rule of law is also tricky since some eastern developing countries may interpret it to mean the respect of the laws and a good judicial system, Japan and most of the developed world will interpret intellectual property rights, and the sanctity of contracts. It is therefore clear that by keeping the language vague Japan is able to openly state its policy position while also avoiding criticism from unresponsive crowds and undemocratic leaders in the developing world. This is a clear example of how the concept of Human Security can be used as a tool for discourse formation. The message in the previous passage is by no means new, but the way to deliver it is. Therefore from a policy perspective the use of Human Security in this instance is very effective in that it helps in the dissemination of beneficial policies in way in which third world sensibilities are not hurt.

Now let us look at the section on sustainable growth. What kind of growth is Japan promoting? Has that changed due to the adoption of the perspective of human security? The next point will easily answer the previous questions by showing that the message has not changed only the language has. First of all, the document uses sustainable growth as a justification for Japan's provision of ODA. "As a country that receives benefits from international trade and that is heavily dependent on other countries for resources, energy, and food, Japan will actively contribute to the sustainable growth of developing countries through ODA. This is highly relevant for ensuring Japan's security and prosperity, thus promoting the interests of the Japanese people" (MOFA, 2005). This passage clearly states the main reason behind Japan's ODA, basically national interest. While the justification provided sounds like any other standard liberal-institutionalist one, it is important to note that it stresses the interdependency of security and thus does reflect the concept of Human Security. It is therefore important to keep an open mind about the core aspects of the concept of human security and remember that some issues that also form part of the neo-liberal agenda can be perfectly compatible with the human security approach.

The section on sustainable growth centers on the promotion of free trade. The document repeatedly states that in addition to providing ODA for economic and social infrastructure it will also provide aid for macroeconomic adjustment including advisors for fiscal and monetary policy (MOFA, 2005). This policy paper clearly states that the main goal should be to promote development through the greater participation of developing countries in the multilateral trading system. It is also worthy of note that the kind of industrial policy that is recommended is private-sector led. In other words by combining a multilateral trading system with a leading private sector the result is an economic policy based on neo-liberal principles. While this is not surprising and by no means negative it is important to understand that while some of the language used in official policy papers such as the one being discussed has changed, the core goals and policies behind it have not. Another important point is that the intended audience of this policy paper is not only the international community but also the Japanese people and thus the Ministry of Foreign Affairs constantly tries to find the right balance between a genuine internationalist commitment to promote development abroad and the imperative of justifying ODA to the Japanese people under difficult economic conditions.

The section following sustainable growth deals with global issues. This section is very vague and broad in nature but mostly concentrates on disaster prevention and environmental problems (MOFA, 2005). While lacking originality the important point about this section is that it stresses the complexity and interconnected nature of disasters and environmental problems. Therefore the solutions proposed are also expected to be complex and comprehensive in nature. The section in discussion simply stresses the importance of allocating ODA for disaster prevention and environmental protection in order to tackle important threats to human security. The language of human security is more obvious here than in the previous section on sustainable growth and helps to highly a tendency for some policy areas to reflect the approach more than others.

The next to last section of the Midterm Policy on ODA deals with the important issue of peace-building. Peace-building is an area that has risen in importance since the Gulf War and continues to be of great importance for international peace and prosperity. In addition to that it has an important psychological effect on the Japanese due to their participation in the first Gulf War and the international criticism it received. As described in earlier chapters of this dissertation, the limitations imposed by the peace constitution mean that Japan's participation in conflict resolution and peace-keeping can be problematic. Thus Japan has tried to find ways around this dilemma by adopting the most up-to-date trends in the field of conflict resolution. One such trend is that of applying the human security approach to peace-keeping, peace-building, and nation building. The Midterm Policy on ODA stresses that all actions taken in the field of peace-building should have a short, mid, and long term perspective (MOFA, 2005). In other words, that all stages of the process should be recognized and connected as part of a whole. One stage should smoothly lead to the next so that reconstruction leads to development for example. In addition to that the paper recognizes that due to the complex nature of conflict the response should also be complex and take into consideration all threats to human security not only those dealing with "freedom from fear" but also those dealing with "freedom from want". This includes promoting development in the former conflict zone so as to improve economic conditions and eliminate the root causes of conflict. The approach recommended by the document also stresses the importance of prevention rather than only intervention after the conflict has already started. Thus this section on peace-building is a good example of a policy area that has been completely absorbed by the human security approach. It includes most of the core precepts of Human Security and uses its language.

The final section of the Midterm Policy on ODA deals with improvements to the process of ODA implementation. This is a section that truly reflects the human security approach in that it stresses the importance of cooperation between stakeholders. Since the three governmental bodies in charge of ODA planning and implementation are the Ministry of Foreign Affairs, the Japan International

Cooperation Agency and up to last year the Japan Bank of International Cooperation the proper coordination and cooperation between them is pivotal for there to be policy coherence and effective implementation of ODA. Thus the Midterm Policy on ODA recommends the establishment of what it calls ODA Task Forces composed of representatives from the three organizations and located in the field (MOFA, 2005). In other words, they will be centered around embassies and will be in charge of recommending and selecting projects for ODA funding. The reason behind this is related to the Human Security approach in that it is believed that by bringing representatives from three different organizations some of which are working at the grassroots level will have a better idea about the needs of the people and most importantly how to appropriately cater to them.

Now let us look back at our description and partial analysis of the 2005 Midterm Policy on ODA. As previously mentioned the lengthy discussion on this government document is due to the pivotal position it plays in term of Japanese ODA policy. The first few sections of the paper almost exclusively deal with human security as a perspective. As previously discussed the introduction uses the language of human security to try to bring cohesion to all other areas of ODA policy such as poverty reduction, and peace-building. It is also important to remember that the paper clearly enumerates specific approaches to ODA as part of the Human Security approach. While most other sections reflect the concept of human security to a certain degree it is evident that it is present throughout the paper. While some sections such as the one on poverty reduction and especially sustainable growth tend to be more conventional in approach. One thing is clear, and that is that the concept of Human

Security is used through out the paper as a way to link previously disparate policy areas and to give ODA a sense of purpose.

4.2.4 The 2006 Diplomatic Bluebook on ODA and Human Security

The 2006 edition of the Diplomatic Bluebook is full of references to the concept of human security while at the same time presents few innovations. The overview of the 2006 edition of the Diplomatic Bluebook clearly states that Human Security has an important position in Japan's foreign policy. In addition to that its subsection on ODA clearly states that Human Security is the central approach guiding its implementation and planning. "In implementing ODA, Japan emphasizes the perspective of 'human security.' Through advocating this concept, Japan aims to create a society that enables each individual to lead a life with dignity. Such goals will be achieved through safeguarding individuals and local communities as well as through building their capacities. Japan is also strengthening cooperation with the NGOs in order to promote the concept of 'human security'" (MOFA, 2006f).

One of the most important introductory sections of the 2006 Diplomatic Bluebook has the subtitle of "Efforts to Tackle Various Global Challenges to Promote Human Security" and while giving a useful introduction on the concept of human security, it concentrates on naming specific actions taken by the Japanese government that fit under the concept of Human Security rather than in explaining the actual approach (MOFA, 2006b). Since this document was explained in detail in previous chapters of this dissertation, at this point it will suffice to say that this paper is mostly descriptive and its value is that is serves as a clear example of how Japan is making an effort to justify not only its ODA policy but all of its foreign policy by means of the human security perspective.

Regarding regional diplomacy, Human Security is also present. In the case of Southeast Asia and more concretely the Association of Southeast Asian Nations (ASEAN), Japan uses the language of Human Security in describing its foreign policy towards this region (MOFA, 2006d). ASEAN is a very important organization for Japan due to the level of economic interdependence and also in terms of conventional security due to geographical proximity. Because of the aforesaid reasons Japan devotes much of its ODA to this region. According to the Ministry of Foreign Affairs 50.6% of the total amount of ODA received by ASEAN is of Japanese origin (MOFA, 2006d). Japan's influence in ASEAN is not limited to ODA but also is exerted through foreign direct investment and other financial flows. While Japan is promoting economic partnerships with those countries it has a vested interest in fostering a stable and safe business environment. This interdependence which is both economic and related to security is captured very well by the concept of human security and because of this Japan has eagerly adopted the approach when describing its foreign policy towards this region. In simple terms Japan's policy is to foster the development of the region and to promote multilateral trade so that both sides of the agreement can prosper and benefit from the relationship. One difference in Japan's policy towards this region compared to the early decades of Japanese ODA is that there is a greater concern for threats to the individual. In other words Japan is showing a greater awareness towards the insecurities caused by market liberalization and other policies related to macro economic adjustment. Safety nets are considered as part of ODA and other aspects such as equity and sustainable development are considered. In other words, one may conclude that while Japan's policy towards Southeast Asia is still centered on trade and economic benefit, there are other aspects that have gained ascendancy such as the protection of vulnerable people from economic downturns and from the negative externalities of industrialization (MOFA, 2006d). Another aspect that is more controversial in nature is Japan's position on human rights and other aspects concerning "freedom from fear". While the ASEAN way is to avoid all kinds of intervention in the internal affairs of member countries, Japan has taken a rather inconsistent approach. Japan maintains in all of its official documents that the promotion of democracy and human rights is a central part of its foreign policy and of the human security approach. The problem is that in practice Japan places economic considerations above political ones and tends to ignore or overlook blatant violations to human rights and fatal blows to democracy such as in the case of the 1996 Military Coup in Thailand. This is incompatible with human security since both "freedom from fear" and "freedom from want" are necessary in order to achieve human security and thus shows that there is a lack of commitment from the Japanese leadership. In other words there is a gap between discourse and implementation.

4.2.5 The Japan International Cooperation Agency and Human Security

"In order to address direct threats to individuals such as conflicts, disasters, infectious diseases, it is important not only to consider the global, regional and national perspectives, but also to consider the perspective of human security, which focuses on individuals. Accordingly, Japan will implement Official Development Assistance (ODA) to strengthen the capacity of local communities through human resource development. To ensure that human dignity is maintained at all stages, from the conflict stage to the reconstruction and development stages, Japan will extend assistance for the protection and empowerment of individuals" (JICA, 2007f).

The Japan International Cooperation Agency is the governmental body in charge of most of the implementation of ODA and recently has assumed the former responsibilities of the Japan Bank of International Cooperation. There are three forms of ODA: yen-loans, technical cooperation, and grant aid. Since this body is in charge of the implementation of the actual projects at the middle and grassroots levels, it is very important to understand how it has adopted the human security approach.

A good starting point is its official policy position paper on Human Security titled "Human Security and JICA" (JICA, 2007a). This paper summarizes the human security approach as embodied by the ODA Charter and the Midterm Policy on ODA (JICA, 2007a). Then it goes on to describe more specific measures espoused by JICA for the proper implementation of ODA.

JICA's view of human security is based on both protection and empowerment. This emphasizes the importance of providing immediate protection to the most vulnerable and at the same time promoting long term sustainable empowerment. This will in turn make the intended beneficiaries more able to withstand sudden downturns and more able to provide for themselves. On a more practical level, JICA states that protection and empowerment should be primarily provided at the community level. The reasoning behind this is that it is between the nation and the individual as a social level. Now we reach an important question. How to provide protection and empowerment? According to JICA it is important to keep in mind that the human security approach should guide both the formulation and the implementation of projects. So as to give some more concrete human security guidelines the policy paper identifies seven basic principles of human security. The first is "reaching those in need through a people-centered approach" (JICA, 2007a). This principle represents the most basic precept of Human Security, namely that security should be centered on the individual not the state. The second principle is "empowering people as well as protecting them". This one reflects a practical approach to the concept of human security that is very useful for ODA implementation. It reflects the holistic and integrated nature of the human security approach. The third principle is "Focusing on the most vulnerable people, whose survival, livelihood and dignity are at risk" (JICA, 2007a). The third principle is also basic to human security in that it places emphasis on helping those who need help the most so as to provide protection before moving on to longer term goals such as development. The fourth principle is "comprehensively addressing both "freedom from want" and "freedom from fear"" (JICA, 2007a). This principle may be interpreted in a variety of ways but it can be understood to mean that both "freedom from want" and "freedom from fear" are necessary in order to achieve human security. Alternatively this reflects the argument over human rights over which set of rights is more important civil and political or economic and cultural. Japan takes a position between those of the Western Powers which favor "freedom from fear" over "freedom from want" and that of the developing world which favors "freedom from want" over "freedom from fear". Thus from this point of view at a theoretical level Japan's point of view on human security may be the most balanced of them all and represents a truly holistic view of human security and of ODA. The fifth principle is "responding to people's needs by assessing and addressing threats through flexible and inter-sectoral approaches" (JICA, 2007a). This principle reflects Japan's flexible stance on human security. Japan favors a flexible definition of the term and a flexible approach that can adapt to changing circumstances and foster the necessary resources and expertise from all sectors of society and all interested stakeholders. This also shows that Japan has a more balanced view than most other opinion groups on human security. While some groups favor the private sector over all other stakeholders, Japan favors a holistic approach that incorporates all sectors and facilitates their cooperation for a common goal, which is to achieve human security. Other groups such as radical NGOs and social movements tend to ignore and demonize the private sector and thus take an antagonistic stance that wastes resources and makes cooperation difficult to say the least. The two final principles also deal with cooperation and they are "Working with both government and local communities to realize sustainable development" and "Strengthening partnerships with various actors to achieve a higher impact from assistance" (JICA, 2007a). The last two principles reiterate the holistic nature of human security. The more actors included the better. Also an aspect of equity between urban and rural development is implied in getting local communities involved. In summary the approach espoused by JICA is one that promotes comprehensive sustainable development and that involves all stakeholders in order to achieve human security.

As described in the previous paragraph, JICA espouses the general guidelines set out in the ODA Charter and the Midterm Policy on ODA but also has its own more specific approach to ODA implementation. The official position on Human Security espoused by JICA is one that is based on protection and empowerment and that gives equal value to "freedom from fear" as to "freedom from want". In addition to that JICA emphasizes the need to get as many stakeholders involved as possible and to keep a flexible approach based on strengthening security at both the national and at the community level.

It is evident that Human Security is overwhelmingly present in JICA's policy on ODA implementation but the question is how is it putting those principles into practice? This was done through four main actions. The first action takes place at the macro level and deals with incorporating human security in JICA's regional and country aid policies (JICA, 2007a). This is an example of a concrete case in which Japan is applying the human security approach for policy formulation at the macro level. The second action is related to reflecting human security in projects and programs. This is a direct statement of intend and wanted to incorporate the human security approach into project formulation and implementation. The third action is improving development instruments and implementation procedures. This deals with how to implement actual projects and shows that the human security approach is followed at all levels of ODA policy from macro level regional policies to village level implementation. This last action deals with assessment and monitoring and attempts to more effectively determine the needs of the people and whether a project has been effective or not. The final action deals with the mainstreaming of the concept of human security. JICA wants to promote the adoption of the approach through contacts and cooperation with NGOs, other donors, international organizations, among others. This last point is important in that JICA explicitly states its intend to promote the concept in other to move it to the mainstream of development discourse. This is a process of discursive construction in which Japan is actively attempting to mainstream its version of human security in order to validate its foreign policy in the eyes of the international community.

CHAPTER V

ODA CASE STUDIES AND HUMAN SECURITY

5.1 Overview

Case studies are important in that they provide specific examples of ODA. By taking a look at some representative ODA projects it will be possible to assess the degree in which the human security approach has affected ODA policy implementation. One of the research objectives of this dissertation was to compare Japan's official discourse to actual implementation of ODA policy and assistance through the UN Fund for Human Security and JICA. The previously mentioned objective will be done in the following sections by means of a discourse analysis of the reports provided by JICA regarding some of the projects that have been carried out with the help of Japanese ODA. Those projects will be judged according to the criteria set out by the Japanese government itself, that is Japan's view of human security. In other words, what will be tested here is not the actual impact of the projects themselves but rather whether the version of human security espoused by JICA and other government bodies was actually present in their formulation and implementation. The present study takes this original approach in that policy coherence is an oftentimes ignored area of public policy and of development studies. The previously described exercise will also be useful in order to determine to what extend the concept of human security has had an impact on Japanese ODA policy making and implementation.

5.2 JICA Case Studies

    5.2.1 Myanmar (Burma)

    Myanmar is a controversial case when talking about Official Development Assistance. It is a state ruled by a military junta with a dark past regarding human rights and democracy. Most Western Democracies refuse to deal with Myanmar until there is a regime change and consider any aid given to this secretive junta to be counterproductive and to have the effect of retarding a possible transition to democracy. On the other hand, authoritarian states such as The People's Republic of China concentrate on economic opportunities and disregard human rights considerations and thus have developed close relations with Myanmar. Japan is an interesting case in that it takes a middle approach towards Myanmar. It does not renounce lucrative economic opportunities but at the same time it uses the rhetoric of human rights and human security.

    The argument used by Japan is not new and echoes earlier debates on economic sanctions and the human cost they involve. In other words, some Nordic States and Japan argue that economic sanctions are counterproductive and against human dignity since the ones affected the most by them are not those in power but rather the most vulnerable. Therefore they favor limited engagement in which NGOs working at the grassroots level are supported in order to try to reach the most vulnerable while avoiding strengthening the oppressive regime in power. Japan and its supporters consider this approach to be more compatible with human security than a hard line approach involving economic sanctions and a complete disengagement due to its emphasis on providing protection and also by fostering long term growth at the grass roots level. Critics point out that an improvement in living conditions may reduce opposition to the regime and thus lengthen the transition period to democracy. In more technical terms, an improvement may bring increased legitimacy to the regime.

Myanmar remains one of the most authoritarian states in the world and also has a very low level of human development. Nevertheless Myanmar has scored a few victories such as in its admission into ASEAN and in the continued assertion of the so called ASEAN way which provides a shield with which to protect itself from criticism and most importantly from external interference in its internal affairs.

At this point it will be useful to look at a specific case study in order to assess whether Japan's approach to Official Development Assistance is truly compatible with the concept of human security. The case in question is that of the Technical Cooperation Project for the Eradication of Opium Poppy Cultivation and Poverty Reduction in Kokang Special Region No. 1 (JICA, 2007b). This project was undertaken in Myanmar's Shan state. This region had an armed conflict with the central government for many years in order to achieve greater autonomy. In 2003 a cease-fire was finally achieved and in exchange for greater autonomy, the region was asked to ban opium poppy plantation. The impact of this prohibition was not only economic but also social. Due to the economic and social isolation of the region, poppy plantation was the most common occupation of the population. Therefore the decision to ban the practice left the majority of the population without a means to earn a living. The previously mentioned ban created great human insecurity and required a comprehensive response in order to be tackled.

This is where a joint project between the government of Myanmar and the Japan International Cooperation Agency came in. The intended plan was supposed to reflect the human security approach and to provide a long term solution for the region. The five year plan started in 2004 and had the goal of providing comprehensive assistance. The main objectives of the project as described by JICA were to "promote social development, including agricultural development (buckwheat cultivation and other substitute crops), infrastructure development, and satisfaction of basic human needs (such as education and health) in the Kokang Special Region of Shan State in northeastern Myanmar" (JICA, 2007b). The initial phase of the project reached 117,000 people and involved aspects of education, crop substitution, and small scale infrastructure (JICA, 2007b). The main idea behind the project was to provide the population with an alternative way of earning a living and for it to be sustainable. The previously mentioned goal was to be reached without sacrificing the most vulnerable in the short term in order to achieve long term goals. So this project had an aspect of protection as well as of empowerment.

Now let us analyze this project through the eyeglass of human security. The first question that comes to mind is whether it is a people-centered project. In this respect the project can be said to comply with the human security approach in that it is people-centered. Its goal is to try to cater to the needs of the population and to deal with their individual problems rather than with more macro economic considerations. Another aspect would be whether it places an emphasis on those who are most vulnerable. The project in discussion does concentrate on those who are most vulnerable and makes an effort to provide not only long term empowerment but also short term protection from the sudden economic downturn caused by the ban on poppy plantation. Another aspect of human security is a comprehensive and inter-sectoral response to threats. This project involves aspects of education, health, agriculture, and others. In addition to that local, national, and international stakeholders are involved in the project. The central government jointly coordinated the project with JICA and the assistance of several community organizations was requested. Thus this project reflects this important aspect of the human security approach. The final aspect of the human security approach dealing with a comprehensive tackling of "freedom from want" and "freedom from fear" is the one that is controversial. While JICA claims that this project addresses both "fear" and "want" it is arguable whether the "fear" aspect is truly considered. The project report makes no mention of human rights nor do the objectives. Those are two important factors behind "freedom from fear". The reason behind that blatant omission of such an important aspect is most likely pressure from the government of Myanmar. Due to this no mention is made of rights in any of their forms, nor of liberties and freedoms. Therefore taking all of those points into consideration one may conclude that this JICA-sponsored project in Myanmar concentrates mostly on tackling "freedom from want" while mostly ignoring "freedom from fear". Furthermore this project shows that Japan is willing to compromise on vital aspects of human security such as human rights when dealing with uncompromising authoritarian states such as Myanmar. In addition to that due to Japan's foreign policy imperatives in having a smooth and harmonious relationship with ASEAN, Japan tends to apply a double standard when it comes to disbursing ODA. Finally, this case study of Japan's ODA policy towards Myanmar shows that in practice Japan's ODA policy favors "freedom from want" over "freedom from fear" and thus does not represent a truly complete human security approach.

5.2.2 Thailand

Japan has a very close economic relationship with Thailand. This Southeast Asian state underwent rapid economic growth through the 90s until it became the epicenter of the 97-98 Financial Crisis. With booming tourism and industrial sectors, Thailand is one of the economic powerhouses of ASEAN. The high degree of economic interdependence between Japan and Thailand should be taken into consideration when looking at its ODA policy towards this country. It should also be noted that since Thailand has reached a relatively good level of economic development, Japan has removed it from the list of its main ODA recipients. Instead Japan aims to establish a strong economic partnership with Thailand. Nevertheless there is still some degree of Official Development Assistance provided to Thailand, mostly in the form of grant aid. Also, due to Thailand's central position in ASEAN it serves as the headquarters of several important aid organizations and region-wide projects. This is the case of the Project that will be discussed in this section.

The case in point is the Asia-Pacific Development Center on Disability. The previously mentioned Center is located in Bangkok and serves the entire Southeast Asian region. It is operated by the Ministry of Social Development and Human Security which is funded by grant aid from Japan. Its goal is to empower disabled people and to build a "barrier-free society" (JICA, 2007d). The Center tackles both physical and non-physical barriers and thus takes a comprehensive approach to the threats faced by disabled people. While the description provided by JICA is vague and ambiguous, from a discourse analysis point of view, it is important to note that it made an effort to use the language of Human Security to justify this project. The Center claims to use three methods in order to achieve its goal. The first is to promote cooperation among the government, NGOs, and others. The second method is to improve access to information for disabled people. And finally, the third method, is to promote the development of human resources in order to help disabled people help themselves. The Center trains disabled people to become leaders and to start their own projects. In addition to that, JICA sends disabled Japanese experts to train future leaders. This project takes a mid to long term perspective based on empowerment.

The ambitious nature of this project reflects the human security approach in that it does not concentrate on an specific threat to disabled people but rather takes a more comprehensive and holistic point of view that attempts to improve their lives. The Center also argues that disabled people represent one of the most vulnerable groups in developing countries and that helping them should therefore be a priority. In this respect this project satisfies the "helping the most vulnerable first" criteria of the human security approach. On the other hand the emphasis on self-help and mid to long term results gives primacy to empowerment over protection. In other words, this project seems to ignore the immediate needs of the disabled. Even though this seems to be reasonable from a feasibility perspective, it is not compatible with the human security approach. From this perspective those disabled people who are most vulnerable at this moment in time should be protected concurrently to taking actions for mid to long term development. Nevertheless there is an important characteristic of this project that makes it highly compatible to the human security approach and that is that it does not confine itself to any specific borders. In other words, it recognizes that the problems faced by disabled people are not limited to a certain country and therefore the Center deals with projects in the entire Asia-Pacific region. It is important to note how this intrudes into the internal affairs of countries but since the issue is not a controversial one, it is not opposed by the atavistic and retrograde elites of the region in question. Thus this is a good starting point in that it sets an example of how official development assistance and development as a whole should be carried out, without limiting the project to national boundaries and certainly not to outdated concepts such as national sovereignty. The project truly reflects human security's core which is a duty to protect and to empower individuals regardless of jurisdiction or geographical location.

5.2.3 Cambodia

Cambodia is a country that has undergone a long period of armed conflict. Due to this its human capital decreased dramatically and its legal system was left in total disarray. After peace was restored in Cambodia, the international community undertook the difficult responsibility of nation-building. Most organs of the government had to be created from scratch and the judicial system needed to be reformed. This large undertaking included training judges, and other legal workers and the actual drafting of the Civil Code and Code of Civil Procedure. In addition to that the population in general had to be reacquainted with a functioning legal system based on the rule of law. This included increasing awareness on human rights and legal procedures to enforce them. In order to tackle aspects of accessibility, advances on legal fees were provided, and local NGOs involved in similar projects were supported. All of the previously described activities were undertaken with the help of

JICA. This project of technical cooperation started in 1999 and through its duration it collaborated with Cambodian and Japanese experts in the drafting of more than 500 articles of the Civil Code and more than a 1000 of the Code of Civil Procedure (JICA, 2007c).

The sheer magnitude of this project makes assessment on terms of results difficult to say the least but since in this study we are interested in the application of the human security approach to development that is not an issue. In term of human security, this project deals with one of the leading trends in the field, nation building. Japan was involved in the entire process of conflict resolution and peace building in Cambodia and this project is an example of one of the most important stages of the process, institution building. The project takes a comprehensive perspective to ODA in that frequently ignored aspects such as institutional reform are tackled. In this case, a responsible member of the international community, is taking an active role in the solution of the internal affairs of Cambodia. In this case, national sovereignty was not a problem due to the peculiar nature of Cambodia at the time thus the pervasive problem of Southeast Asia, nationalism, was momentarily under control. In addition to that starting from scratch was a perfect opportunity in order to apply the most advanced trend in development and the best government institutions possible. Without the problem of having to reform preexisting outdated institutions, Cambodia became the flagship development project of the international community.

The technical cooperation project in discussion is interesting in that it is a case in which ODA was used for the purpose of improving an intangible asset rather than in a huge infrastructure project. In addition to that judicial reform is highly intrusive and political and therefore sets a precedent in that the international community not only has the right but also the duty to interfere in building institutions conducive to the achievement of human security. In this case Japan tackled not only "freedom from want" but also "freedom from fear" and thus showed that at least in non-confrontational instances like judicial reform in Cambodia, it is willing to apply an important side of human security which is that related to "freedom from fear". Thus this project of judicial reform is a comprehensive solution that both protects and empowers the Cambodian population in the short, mid, and long terms.

In conclusion while this project is a good example of Japan taking human security seriously as an approach to ODA planning and implementation, it also shows that its application is opportunistic. While human rights and the rule of law were not mentioned in the case of ODA to Myanmar they were the center piece in the case of Cambodia. This is a clear sign of an inconsistent application of the human security approach.

5.2.4 Indonesia

Indonesia has had a turbulent relationship with Japan. It had an ambivalent colonial experience in which Japan "liberated" it from Dutch rule and later imposed its own rule. However the important point about that period was that Japan was promoting its East Asia Co-prosperity Sphere with rhetoric of "Asia for the Asians" and thus served as an earlier attempt at empowerment. After WWII Japan paid reparations to Indonesia and quickly increased its economic interdependency with the Southeast Asian archipelago. Indonesia's affiliation with the non-aligned movement during much of the cold-war prevented close political ties from developing but it did not stop Japan's thirst for raw materials and Indonesia desire for consumer products (Trinidad, 2007).

This section will look at two projects funded by Japanese Official Development Assistance in Indonesia. The first project is a good example of development at the macro level (national level) promoting the human security approach. The title of this project was Community Empowerment Project with Civil Society (PKPM). PKPM started in 2004 as a three year-long venture (JICA, 2007e). The project was implemented in Indonesia's 10 eastern provinces, which were chosen due to their low level of development and high levels of poverty compared to the rest of the country. The project in discussion was undertaken with the cooperation of Indonesia's National Development Planning Agency as a means to promote a participatory approach to development. This goal was to be achieved through the provision of workshops on participatory development and other related approaches for local government officials, national government officials, and community leaders. The workshops were supposed to help engender support for local development initiatives at the community level.

Now let us put this project to the human security test. The first and most important principle of human security is that it is individual centered. It is clear that this project does not satisfy that criteria since it is community centered and this means that while a participatory development approach may have some things in common with the human security approach they differ in their most important tenet. Human Security clearly states that the referent is the individual and that the needs of the individual should be placed above that of the community. On the other hand, the participatory approach, especially as practiced in Asia and as depicted by this project, is community based. A second criterion of the human security approach is that it aims to protect the most vulnerable first. In this respect, this project does follow the human security approach since it was first implemented in the ten poorest provinces of the country and was expected to spread from there. A third criterion is that of empowerment and ownership. The project does contain many elements that promote ownership and one of the major goals of it is to promote community initiatives. The project aims to train government officials to be responsive to the needs of the community and to collaborate with them in order to implement community initiatives for development. The Human Security approach is also compatible with the cross-sectoral nature of the project. It involves representatives from both national and local government, NGOs, community leaders, and international organizations. Therefore this aspect of the project is compatible with the Human Security approach.

So is PKPM a true example of the human security approach put into practice with the support of Japanese Official Development Assistance? The answer to this question is not clear. There are aspects of the previous project that are perfectly compatible with most aspects of the human security approach but there seems to be a different ethos to this project as compared to the other ones analyzed in previous sections. The evidence for the previous assertions is that the language used shows a slight but significant variation when compared to that of other projects that were clearly planned following the human security approach such as the one dealing with Judicial reform in Cambodia. PKPM uses a language reflecting earlier and sometimes parallel trends in development such as participatory development and community-based development which have, as of late, being adapted to the Human Security approach by some practitioners. Nevertheless on a theoretical level they differ on core tenets when compared to a pure version of human security. Participatory development and community-based development place more emphasis on local development and on the protection of the community above all else while giving less emphasis to political and civil rights and to democracy at the national level. Furthermore it should be remembered that the main difference between them is that human security places emphasis on the individual and the community is just another level of human association. In conclusion the PKPM project is compatible with a loose version of Asianized human security but it is not an offspring of the human security approach but rather an adapted project molded to fit the currently prevailing trend. It should be noted that the main point here is not whether the project is compatible with human security nor whether it is effective or not, but rather what is its theoretical origin.

Now let us look at a second project, this project shares some of the aims of the previously analyzed one but deals with individual participation rather than only at the village level as the previous one. The Technical Cooperation Project for Community Development Based on Citizen Participation has the aim of promoting local development through individual initiatives and citizen participation in the fields of basic healthcare, basic education, the improvement of living standards, and the development of small-scale community infrastructure. The project aims to train citizens from all walks of life to participate in local development and to engage in capacity building. Local citizens are encouraged to work together with provincial government in order to plan and implement development initiatives. It is important to note that other than in the title the word "community" is scantily used and the word "citizen" is preferred. The level of government to which there is more frequent mention is the provincial one and the name given to the approach of this project is citizen participatory approach. Finally, the overall goal of this project is "to create a framework for bottom-up development based on the implementation of projects that truly reflect the needs of people, and to extend that framework progressively to other regions" (JICA, 2007e).

It is evident that there are some important similarities between the two projects implemented in Indonesia. They both promote a participatory approach but while the first promotes a community based participatory approach, the second favors a citizen based participatory approach. The second project of Technical cooperation also tries to concentrate on four basic areas that are considered to be of importance to deal with vulnerable people. This reflects the vulnerability aspect of human security. This project also shows a large content of empowerment and ownership. Its aim is to promote local initiatives and participation which are both conducive to ownership and to empowerment. Therefore in that respect, this project also reflects the human security approach. The cross-sectoral collaboration criterion is also satisfied due to the involvement of a varied range of stakeholders from all levels. Finally the most important theoretical criterion is also satisfied, that is it is people centered. The emphasis on the role of the individual citizen is a true reflection of the human security approach. Thus in summary the Technical Cooperation Project for Community Development Based on Citizen Participation does reflect the human security approach to development.

In conclusion the two projects implemented in Indonesia do show important aspects of the human security approach. While the first reflects an approach more compatible with other trends such as community-based participatory development or sufficiency economy, the second is more theoretically compatible with human security due to its citizen/individual centered approach. The two projects nevertheless lack an important aspect of human security and that is "freedom from fear". They do not make any mention of political freedom nor of any other political or civil rights and rather concentrate on economic and social aspects. The reasons behind this are varied but a major one is probably Indonesia's, and for that matter the region's, mistaken nationalism and the primacy played by the principle of sovereignty. In other words, "freedom from want" is less controversial and is perceived to be less intrusive by recipient countries than projects dealing with "freedom from fear", thus Japan probably opted for the former so as to maintain a harmonious relationship with the resource-rich ASEAN member. It is evident from the previous chapters that this is inconsistent with Japan's twin policy regarding human security. Most important policies papers regarding Human Security and ODA maintain that both "freedom from want" and "freedom from fear" are vital parts of the human security approach and the two examples of Japanese ODA in Indonesia fail to show any mention of "freedom from fear".

5.2.5 Vietnam

Vietnam is a country that has not had historically close relations with Japan due to its affiliation with the communist block during the cold war. However this started to change after the Doi Moi policy of opening up the country to a market-based economy. As shown in Table 4 of the present dissertation, Japan is providing increasingly large amounts of ODA to Vietnam in the form of loans. This shows Japans interest in the rising Southeast Asian economy and trust in its ability to pay back the loans incurred (Trinidad, 2007). Vietnam continues to be one of the last actually existing communist countries in the world and one of the last three in Asia.

Due to this, projects related to civil and political rights are limited by an authoritarian government. In other to circumvent this possible stones along the way towards a mutually beneficial economic partnership, Japan has placed an emphasis on the "freedom from want" aspect of human security when dealing with Official Development aid to Vietnam. The following case study is a clear example of one such project that ignores the "freedom from fear" aspect of the human security approach.

Reproductive Health Project in Nghe An Province started in 1996 in one of the poorest and most remote regions of Vietnam. This region is inhabited by hill tribe peoples who are among the most vulnerable in an already poor country. The 3 million inhabitants of this province tended to have very poor health coverage before 1996 and less than 60% of pregnant women gave birth in health centers (JICA, 2007g). The previously mentioned state of affairs represented a high health risk for the mothers and the unborn children and therefore the Reproductive Health Project promoted the establishment of an administrative service system covering health care needs of mothers and infants and also supported capacity building for those involved in health related education. This was done by the dispatch of experts, volunteers, and by the building of the necessary infrastructure by means of grant aid. A management committee composed of "representatives from among local residents, the government, community groups, and the healthcare sector at the provincial, county, and communal levels" was formed to direct the project (JICA, 2007g).

The project in discussion protects the most vulnerable first as seen by the choice of implementing the project in one of the most remote and poor regions of Vietnam. In addition to that, the project concentrates on one of the most vulnerable subgroups, women and children, and their health. By doing this, the Reproductive

Health Project reflects and important aspect of human security. The human security approach to ODA is also present in the management of the project which is composed by a cross-sectoral panel representing most stakeholders. An additional aspect to be noted is that Japanese volunteers were also deployed so as to tackle the problem at the grassroots level. In other words, the project takes a comprehensive and holistic approach to the reproductive health problem of the region. Training is provided at all levels and in addition to the provision of the provision of necessary infrastructure through grant aid, empowerment is also promoted through grass roots participatory development. Thus, this project embodies most aspects of human security but at the same time ignores important aspects necessary for achieving complete human security for hill tribe people. One such possible aspect could be related to proper registration of those babies. Another important aspect could be related to minority rights or representation in the national government. Those important aspects of human security are ignored due to practical considerations. In this case the main limiting factor is the authoritarian nature of the Vietnamese government and ASEAN's policy of non-intervention. Therefore Japan prefers to ignore those important aspects of human security in favor of maintaining harmony and of promoting a mutually beneficial economic partnership with Vietnam.

CHAPTER VI

EPISTEMIC SHIFT IN JAPANESE ODA POLICY AND DISCOURSIVE

CO-OPTATION

6.1 Human Security as a Paradigm or *episteme*

It is clear that Human Security is much more than a practical approach to development and that it differs from other related trends in that it is a paradigm that goes beyond the field of development studies and attempts to encompass international relations as a whole. This is a very important point in that it indicates that in order to understand the true importance of Human Security as a paradigm or *episteme* it is necessary to zoom out and see the big picture. Such an ambitious theory claims to have answers to problems ranging from development to traditional security (strategic studies) and thus helps place the development field in perspective. The truly innovative idea introduced by Human Security is the way in which all areas of foreign policy are connected to each other and most importantly are given a common goal to strive for. According to the Human Security paradigm all areas of foreign policy are equally important and are interrelated and interdependent. This means that in order for human security to be achieved there must be policy coherence between the different policy areas. This coherence is achieved by means of co-operation and collaboration between all of the stakeholders in both the planning and the implementation stages of policy making. The comprehensive nature of human security makes it more than just a simple practical approach to development such as needs-based approach, or participatory development but rather represents an attempt at shifting the overarching paradigm in international relations from realism and institutionalist liberalism to human security. The present study has attempted to show how the Human Security paradigm was adopted and promoted by Japan since the late 1990s and how it has affected its foreign policy. ODA policy was chosen as a representative area and the relative impact of the Human Security paradigm was assessed by means of an analysis of official discourse and case studies. This final chapter will attempt to sum up the findings of this study regarding the use of Human Security as a policy tool in official discourse.

6.1.1 Japan's use of Human Security as a Policy Tool in Official Discourse

Figure 1 Discursive Permeation of ODA Policy by the language of Human Security over time

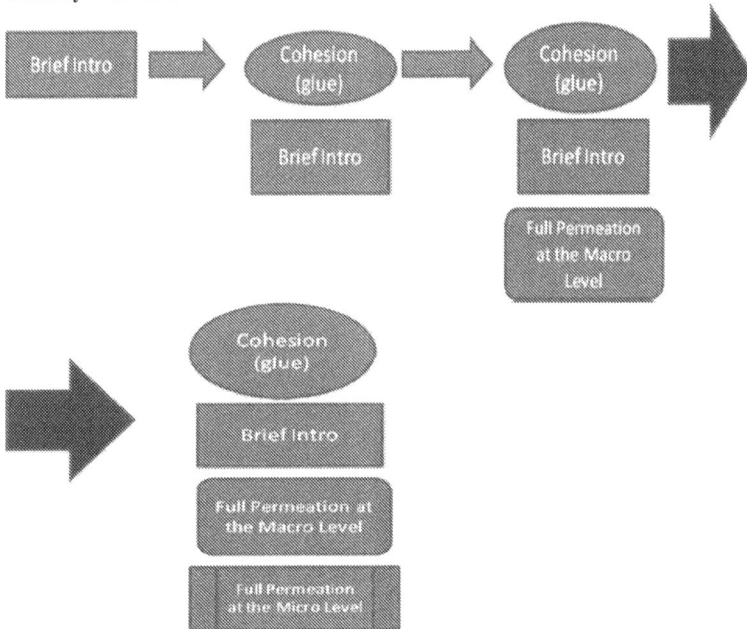

As discussed at length in chapters three and four of this dissertation, Japan has widely used the language of Human Security in its official discourse since the late

1990s. This change reflects a long term process of adaptation of Japan's foreign policy to external conditions. Nevertheless Japan's foreign policy does not necessarily coincide with its official discourse as was evident during most of the Cold War. In other words Japan's official discourse regarding ODA has gone through several stages as discussed in section 4.1. It was originally very functional and blunt and openly promoted Japan's economic interests abroad. However the paradigm present at the time, "developmentalism", did have some uniquely Japanese characteristics. This norm was based on the belief that the economic development of the region would benefit everyone economically including Japan. Thus Japan justified its foreign policy of "economism" by the parallel norm of "developmentalism". This was used in official discourse so as to present an image of coherence and to justify in the eyes of the world its economic policy towards the third world. This paradigm then gave way to common security and even later on to comprehensive security. Those two paradigms served to legitimize Japan's low-posture policy based on trade and "developmentalism". Comprehensive security provided a clear theoretical link between development and peace. Such a theory was perfectly compatible with Japan's non-military role in the international community. Due to Japan's limitation regarding international military participation a paradigm that shifts the emphasis of international security from conventional security (strategic studies) to development and peace building perfectly fit Japan's *de facto* foreign policy. This paradigm suffered a severe blow during the Gulf War after which Japan's foreign policy was judged to be opportunistic by the international community. At this point several factors both internal and external coincided in order to bring Human Security to the forefront of Japanese foreign policy.

Figure 2 "Protective" Human Security vs. "Development" Human Security

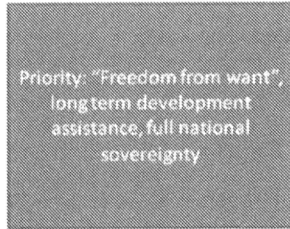

"PROTECTIVE" HUMAN
SECURITY

"DEVELOPMENT" HUMAN
SECURITY

Priority: "Freedom from Fear", responsibility to protect, limited national sovereignty

Priority: "Freedom from want", long term development assistance, full national sovereignty

A growing awareness in the development field that traditional development was not benefiting some sectors of society and in the field of security studies that conventional peace keeping operations were not able to cope with complex humanitarian emergencies were connected by the rising Human Security Paradigm. The fact that most conflicts in the late 20th and early 21st centuries were internal rather than inter-state also helped to emphasize that securing the state was not enough. In addition to that the fact that a large proportion of the most bloody conflicts were ethnic in nature helped destroy the myth of the ideal nation-state based on ethnic and cultural unity. Human Security was able to explain all of those relatively new insecurities at least at the theoretical level by shifting the referent from the state to the individual and the securitizer from the military apparatus of the state to a wide range of concerned stakeholders. Japan seized the opportunity to promote this paradigm as a way to justify its historic emphasis on economic rather than military aid. Furthermore the embryonic paradigm gave middle powers such as Canada, Australia, and Japan the opportunity to take a greater role in international affairs beyond that expected of them based on relative military power. Japan wanted to seize a power which was potentially as powerful as that of the military, and that was the power to set international norms. Norm setting at the international level is a long process that happens gradually by short and sporadic moments of cooperation between states in international fora. Those norms are confined to the space allowed by the prevalent *episteme* or paradigm. Therefore, any new norms are always expected to conform to the prevalent paradigm which serves as the glue that brings cohesion to the international system. The present *episteme* is arguably the Westphalia system of independent nation states and on a more theoretical level the leading paradigm is still realism. It is clear that operation within the confines of the Westphalia system at the practical level and of realism at the theoretical level is disadvantageous for Japan. As a state that has emphasized "economism" and "developmentalism" since the end of World War II it is clear that an analysis of its foreign policy based on realism would be problematic to say the least. It was therefore necessary for Japan to follow two twin approaches to the previously mentioned policy dilemma.

One approach would be the one espoused by realists and neo-realists and would mean that Japan should attempt to become what conservatives call a "normal" country. In other words, for Japan to amend or circumvent the constitutional prohibition on military forces so as to better fit the ideal of the nation-state under the Westphalian system. Needless to say this is an approach that has been followed especially since the Gulf War shock and has reached its peak in recent months with the discussion on an amendment to the Constitution in order to legalize the army. As evidence for this assertion one may mention the notable increase in Japan's participation in peace-keeping and peace-making operations in the last few years.

Figure 3 Twin Approaches to Ruling Paradigm

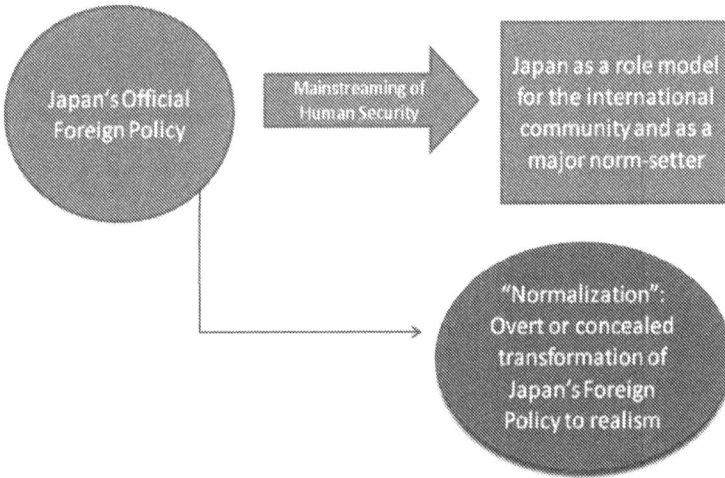

This trend reflects a rise in nationalism and a recovery in the influence of the Liberal Democratic Party in the government. In addition to that external factors such as the United States' pressure on Japan , *beiatsu*, regarding military cooperation in the Asia Pacific region has prompted the government to assume some of the security burden in East Asia. Thus this approach of "normalization" is being promoted by conservative politicians at home and the pressure of Japan's most important ally, the United States. It should be noted at this point that the language used in this approach. "Normalization" implies that there is a set mold to be followed, an ideal. This ideal is a nation-state that possesses armed forces proportionate to its resources and population and that assumes its duty in helping maintain international security through global or regional policing. It is clear that this ideal is that prescribed by realist and neo-realist theorists. Thus this approach of "normalization" is one that attempts to adapt to the prevalent paradigm rather than attempting to shift it in order to attain legitimacy for Japan's foreign policy from the international community.

Figure 4 Sources of Pressure to "normalize"

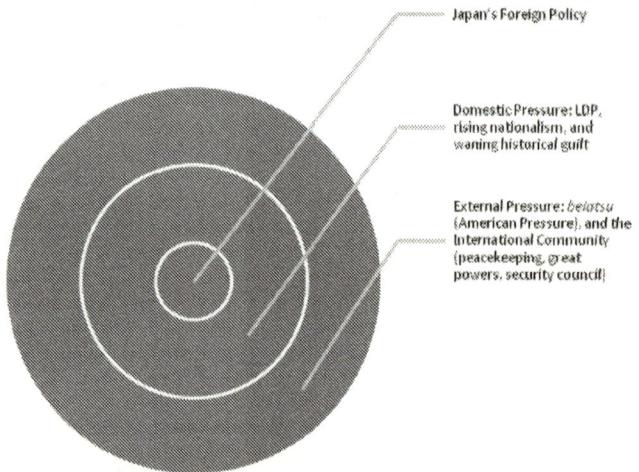

Japan's Foreign Policy

Domestic Pressure: LDP, rising nationalism, and waning historical guilt

External Pressure: *beiatsu* (American Pressure), and the International Community (peacekeeping, great powers, security council)

The second approach is the mainstreaming of the Human Security paradigm. This approach attempts to provoke a paradigmatic shift in order to bring Human Security to primacy and thus face more favorable rules by which to be judged. In other words, this approach attempts to change what is considered normal by the international community in order for it to resemble more closely Japan's traditional foreign policy. As discussed in section 3.6, Human Security is highly compatible with Japan's traditional foreign policy and therefore its rise to primacy would mean that Japan would become an example to be followed rather than a country to be "normalized".

The second approach grows in complexity when one analyses Japan's official discourse and finds that the language of Human Security is also used in order to promote realist and neo-realist policies. However this does not mean that some neo-realist policies are not compatible with Human Security but they differ in their ultimate goal. In the case of Human Security policies should serve to secure the individual while in the case of realism they should serve to secure the state. One more concrete example of this is the growing emphasis on peace-keeping and nation-building. While those two are important aspects of Human Security they tend to be promoted by conservative politicians as a way to sugarcoat the first approach, "normalization". Japan's international responsibility to protect and to empower is used as a way to justify the improvement of the armed forces and the softening of the limits on military cooperation. This is a clear case of discursive co-optation since realist stakeholders are using the language of human security to justify policies that further their goals. Nevertheless the result at the official discourse level does reflect a balanced view of Human Security. As discussed in section 4.2, Japan's official view of Human Security tends to be very balanced compared to other middle powers and civil society organizations. Japan's view of Human Security at the official discourse level presents a picture of perfect balance between "freedom from want" and "freedom from fear" and between "protection" and "development". This is probably due to the pull effect created by the recent neo-realist and neo-liberal wave in Japanese politics and their attempt to make Japan and more "normal" country. This phenomenon helped move Japan's foreign policy along the "want"-"fear" continuum from the far end of the "want" side to the middle. Thus the resulting policy tends to resemble that recommended by the UN Commission on Human Security in its final report, *Human Security Now* (United-Nations, 2003).

6.1.2 Japan's official ODA Policy as an Example of a Paradigmatic Shift

As explained in the previous section, Japan's official foreign policy has gone through a process in which the language of Human Security has been used for two main purposes. The first purpose was to bring cohesion to its foreign policy and to promote the mainstreaming of a favorable paradigm. The second was to promote individual policies which would help further the goal of making Japan a "normal" country without raising internal and external opposition, circumventing historical guilt.

Figure 5 Epistemic Shift from Realism to Human Security

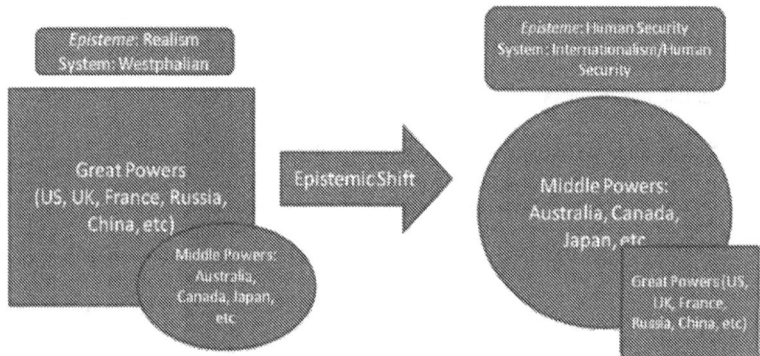

Section 4.2 shows how ODA policy has undergone a process of permeation with the language of human security. This was demonstrated by the detailed analysis of pivotal official policy papers in Chapter IV. Thus it is clear that the Human Security paradigm has had a strong impact on official ODA policy. Its language is

used through most policy papers in order to justify individual policies and in order to bring cohesion to ODA policy as a whole.

The resulting official ODA policy is one that truly reflects the Human Security approach to development and to humanitarian intervention including both protection and empowerment. The latest trends in development are integrated into Japan's official ODA policy as reflected by the 2003 ODA Charter on a macro level and by JICA's Policy Paper on Human Security on a micro level. Nevertheless this ideal picture depicted by official ODA policy is not always reflected by actual ODA funded projects.

6.2 Official Discourse and ODA Case Studies

Chapter five dealt with specific case studies of projects claiming to follow the Human Security approach for ODA. While it is clear that on a discursive level, human security has thoroughly permeated JICA and the language used in its project reports, it is not so clear whether Human Security provided the guiding policy for their formulation and implementation. There are two main problems when assessing Japan's Official ODA discourse regarding Human Security and comparing it to actual case studies. The first is the problem of the chicken and the egg. Which one came first? This is not a major problem when analyzing Japan's Official ODA discourse at the macro level since most important policy documents like the ODA Charter and the Mid-term Policy Paper on ODA were carefully drafted and clearly try to show that Human Security was the guiding paradigm behind them, at least at the discoursive level. Therefore, in this case it is clear that Human Security came first and then the other specific policy areas were molded and adapted to fit the general paradigm. However, this is not so clear when dealing with specific case studies.

When analyzing specific case studies one is able to identify one clear commonality. All reports provided by JICA attempt to use the language of Human Security so as to give them coherence and legitimacy. Nevertheless it is also clear that some projects were formulated having other approaches other than human security in mind and were then sugarcoated with human security language in order to disguise them. This does not mean that the projects reviewed in Chapter V are not compatible with Human Security but rather than some where adapted to fit the language of human security but were inspired by other contemporary approaches in the field of development studies such as sustainable development and participatory development. One such example is the Community Empowerment Project with Civil Society in Indonesia. This project was described and analyzed in detail in section 5.2.4 and it was concluded that it was a clear example of community-based participatory development. This is an approach that is relatively compatible with Human Security but is distinctly different at the theoretical level. Its emphasis on the community over the individual does not present a major obstacle at the practical level but is clearly incompatible at the theoretical level. Simply because if the individual is prioritized by the security label then there should be no need to prioritize the community. And if one community is prioritized then that community is being favored above other groups. In summary, this project is an example of how some case studies represent projects inspired by different development approaches and then adapted to fit the language of human security.

A second problem encountered while analyzing specific case studies of the use of Human Security in Japanese funded ODA projects was that some projects tended to place more emphasis on "freedom from want" than on "freedom from fear". It is clear from the 2003 ODA Charter that Japan connects ODA to respect for human rights and to democracy. Section 4.2.2 on the ODA Charter clearly shows how there is a principle of conditionality similar to that of the Western Powers which attempts to use ODA as a tool to promote "freedom from fear". This important aspect of Human Security is often ignored when dealing with rogue states such as Myanmar and with regions with a high regard for national sovereignty such as South East Asia.

Economic considerations continue to have precedence over political ones in the eyes of the Japanese government. This can be observed clearly in the cases of Japan's ODA Policy towards countries like Myanmar and Vietnam. Both countries have authoritarian governments with a dark past regarding human rights violations. Due to the economic importance of ASEAN for the Japanese economy, considerations regarding human rights and the spread of democracy are put aside in favor of national interest. An attempt is made to justify this by connecting development to long term peace and the gradual transformation of authoritarian regimes to democracies. In other words, Japan justifies its ODA to those states by stressing the importance of a peaceful and gradual move towards democracy rather than by confrontation. In addition to that Japan has to navigate the dangerous waters of Southeast Asian nationalism. The colonial period left the region stuck in what Fukuyama calls "history" and thus the political trends encountered reflect those of Europe in the 19th and early 20th centuries (Fukuyama, 1992). That factor combined to Japan's historical guilt make it very difficult for Japan to press on issues of human rights and democracy. ASEAN has also made it clear that its way is to avoid intervention in the internal affairs of member countries and the promotion of economic cooperation.

Projects undertaken in Myanmar and Vietnam lack any mention of human rights or of democratic participation and tend to concentrate on tackling "freedom from want" as a means to promote mutually beneficial economic partnerships. In the case of Myanmar the Technical Cooperation Project for the Eradication of Opium Poppy Cultivation and Poverty Reduction in Kokang Special Region No. 1 is a clear example of a cooperation with an authoritarian government in order to tackle "freedom from want" while obviating "freedom from fear".

There are some cases in which Japan does attempt to tackle "freedom from fear" but usually only in cases in which there is little to no opposition from the beneficiary. This is the case of Cambodia and of the Project of Judicial Reform. Due to the peculiarly propitious circumstances present in Cambodia at the time, Japan and the international community were able to put into practice the Human Security approach for nation-building. This is a case in which both "freedom from fear" and "freedom from want" were tackled and given equal emphasis.

Most other projects fall in between the cases previously described. Japan is clearly attempting to implement the human security approach but has opted for adapting to external circumstances. In other words, the approach has had to adapt to the realities and exigencies of *real politik*. It is also clear that Japan's ODA is becoming more strategic as a tool for promoting Japan's economic foreign policy.

Table 5 Japan's ODA Policy on Paper and in Practice

Japan's ODA Policy's Components	Official ODA Policy	ODA recipient: *nationalist, high regard for national sovereignty*	ODA recipient: *Internationalist or in the process of nation building*
Conditionality based on Human Rights and Democracy	Yes	No	Yes
Promotion of free market policies	Yes	Yes	Yes
Attempts to tackle "freedom from want"	Yes	Yes	Yes
Attempts to tackle "freedom from fear"	Yes	No	Yes
Resulting Policy:	*Human Security*	*"developmentalism", truncated version of Human Security*	*Human Security*

Note: The present table summarizes results from case studies.

6.3 21st Century Official Development Assistance Policy Apologetics and Discursive Co-optation

Apologetics is a field of theology developed by the Roman Catholic Church in order to study how to defend and legitimize the teachings of the Church. The methods used to defend the Church at a theoretical level are very similar to those used by governments in official discourse. The first step is always to attempt to set the ruling paradigm by which everything else will be judged. The Church was able to do this for several centuries by means of developing complex paradigms such as divine and natural law and by having Doctors of the Church like St. Thomas Aquinas writing treatises connecting all areas of life to those central tenets. In other words, the main purpose of those treatises was to promote the mainstreaming of the paradigm in addition to providing legitimacy to specific Church practices.

This process of apologetics was eagerly adopted by many other fields and institutions one of which was states. In an age of democratic accountability and more recently international responsibility it is necessary for a government to publicly defend its policies. A State must publicly announce the goal of its policies and the process by which they were formulated and implemented. This is the case of foreign policy which is a unique field in that a policy must gain national and international legitimacy to be considered successful. Thus the dilemma of reconciling national interest with international responsibility is brought to the fore for the first time in political science.

This study has used an specific policy field in order to show in detail how the process of what I call 21st Century Policy Apologetics takes place. A State adopts a beneficial paradigm and attempts to promote its acceptance by the international community. This process of mainstreaming is expected to ultimately lead to a shift in paradigms or *epistemes* from which the promoting state gains legitimacy and norm setting power.

The field of international relations is currently contested by several paradigms ranging from realism to critical theory and human security. Those paradigms compete against each other for primacy and most importantly for the recognition of policy makers. This is the path from the University to the Capitol. Currently the two most widely accepted and influential paradigms are neo-realism and institutional liberalism.

Those two paradigms more closely resemble the foreign policies of the great powers. This in turn prompts middle powers and developing countries to promote their own paradigms in order to legitimize their own foreign policies and world views. This was the case of dependency theory by the third world and is currently the case of Japan and Canada with Human Security.

It is therefore natural for middle powers such as Japan to try to mainstream a paradigm that favors their foreign policy. Japan has done this through its support for comprehensive security in the 1980s and later on by its adoption of Human Security. The twin norms of "economism" and "developmentalism" gain legitimacy through the theoretical glue of Human Security. Policies previously called "opportunistic" can be renamed human security friendly. Most importantly Japan's overall foreign policy can be re-assessed through the paradigm of Human Security and thus be able to gain international recognition and possibly a leadership position. This is clear in Japan's attempt to promote the reform of the UN Security Council in the early 21st Century and the use of Human Security language as a way to claim recognition for its contribution to international peace and security.

Figure 6 Japan's Well-balanced view of Human Security in Theory

-Priority: Both "freedom from want" and "freedom from fear"
- Responsibility to protect and to provide long term development assistance
- theoretically limited national sovereignty when dealing with the "market" and "human rights" (ODA Conditionality)

As described throughout this dissertation, policy making is a complex process involving many stakeholders and factors. It is therefore important to remember that governments are not unitary actors but their actions represent the final result of a tug-o-war between competing policies and factions. Japan's ODA Policy is no exception to this and thus it is clear that its Official ODA Policy is a result of complex negotiations and interactions between stakeholders both inside and outside Japan responding to their national and international environment.

Discursive Co-optation is the process in which policies are disguised by means of official discourse in order to make them more acceptable for the public both at home and abroad. The case in point is that of conservative politicians of the Liberal Democratic Party promoting the "normalization" of Japan by means of official discourse that uses the language of Human Security. "Normalization" refers to a neo-realist ideal that favors the legalization of the armed forces and the softening of the ban on international military cooperation while Human Security refers to the protection and empowerment of the individual. The goal behind neo-realist policies should always be the security of the state and the relative increase in power of the state in question in the international system. On the contrary the goal behind the Human Security paradigm is the attainment of human security for all individuals regardless of geographic location. It is clear that the methods used to achieve those two different goals may coincide as in the case of peace-keeping operations and nation-building but it is also clear that the final goals are different. Therefore in the case of Japanese ODA Policy, conservative politicians have identified the opportunity of using the language of Human Security in order to promote certain policies which are compatible with both paradigms. However it is clear that by using the language of

Human Security they are trying to misguide the public and the international community regarding their true intentions and final goal. Thus, this is a clear case of discursive co-optation. The discourse of Human Security has been and is still being co-opted by neo-realist elements in the Japanese government who share the goal of making Japan a "normal" country in the neo-realist sense.

Table 6 Discursive Co-optation of Human Security in Japan's ODA Policy

Overarching Theory	Willingness to tackle "freedom from want"	Willingness to tackle "freedom from fear"	Willingness to increase Japan's cooperation in peace-building	Language used in Official Policy	Goal
Neo-realist stakeholders	Yes	When convenient	Yes	Human Security	"Normalization" of Japan
Human Security Approach	Yes	Yes	Yes	Human Security	Achievement of Human Security

6.4 "Earning" versus "Spending"

A common way of defining an ODA policy is the dichotomy of "earning" vs. "spending". While helpful in describing the major characteristics of ODA as a strategy it oversimplifies the complex nature of ODA policy. Trinidad makes the case in his paper on the disbursement of Japanese ODA to Southeast Asia that Japan is moving towards a "spending" strategy (Trinidad, 2007). He bases this assertion on a quantitative study of Japan's ODA from 1991 to 2004. While some of the conclusions he reaches form his analysis are backed by strong quantitative evidence others tend to be logical jumps. One example of this is that while Trinidad shows that Japan has progressively allocated more ODA in the form of grants rather than loans he tend to equate those grants with humanitarian intentions. In other words, Trinidad equates "spending" strategies with humanitarian concerns and altruism. The logical jump takes place from identifying an increased "spending" strategy with humanitarian intentions and altruism. Thus, while several important trends identified by Trinidad such as Japan's increasingly strategic use of ODA due to domestic pressure under strict budgetary constraints and more sparing use grant aid for nation-building are valid and rest on solid empirical and cognitive ground, his final conclusion and especially his forecast do not. Trinidad claims that Japan's ODA is moving towards a "spending" strategy which he equates with altruism and humanitarian concerns as opposed to "earning" and geoeconomic concerns (Trinidad, 2007). In the present dissertation I have shown the exact opposite. That while Japan claims to follow humanitarian concerns in the form of the concept of Human Security, it continues to follow geoeconomic and geopolitical concerns as the driving force behind its ODA Policy. Finally, it was clearly shown that the empirical evidence provided by quantitative data of Japan's ODA from 1991 to 2004 conform to the theoretical model presented by the present dissertation. Furthermore, the logical leap taken by Trinidad in his quantitative analysis of Japanese ODA to Southeast Asia is complemented by a detailed discursive analysis of Japan's Official ODA Discourse and predicts a very different landing for Japan's future ODA policy. In conclusion "spending" and "earning" strategies do not represent a perfect dichotomy and may be used interchangeably to further geoeconomic and geopolitical goals.

6.5 An Uncertain Path towards Human Security

It is unclear at this point whether Human Security will attain primacy over competing paradigms. However, the paradigm has already had a deep impact in the fields of humanitarian aid and development assistance. This is partly due to the role played by middle powers like Japan and the Nordic Countries in those fields. The all-encompassing nature of the paradigm is one of its most alluring qualities while also one of its most important weaknesses.

Attacks at the paradigm come from two main fronts. From an academic point of view, the paradigm presents some major flaws and incongruities such as those identified by MacFarlane and Khong who go as far a as excluding economic security as part of Human Security (Khong, 2006). Another front is that of practitioners and stakeholders, otherwise known as the real world. In this front the most common attack is on the actual value of the approach for policy making. Its all encompassing and vague-nature make it difficult to use for policy making and implementation. While at the same time that same vagueness gives it the necessary flexibility to garner the support of a varied group of stakeholders

The strong point of the Human Security paradigm is how it connects the local to the global and most importantly how it shifts the emphasis of security from the state to the individual. Therefore, the power of this paradigm may not be its theoretical traction but rather its ideological pull. Human Security resembles a philosophy more than a theory of international relations not only in its normative basis but also in its all encompassing nature.

Japan's foreign policy has and will continue to be influenced by this rising paradigm but whether Human Security will stay with us long enough to reach primacy over neo-realism is another story. It is clear that it has impacted some policy areas more than others and that while official discourse tends to reflect the paradigm most policy makers remain skeptical and uncommitted to its most basic tenets.

REFERENCES

Aoi, Y. Y. a. C. (2000). Chapter 5: Japan's foreign policy towards human rights: Uncertain changes, *Columbia International Affairs Online* (pp. 45-78).

Aso, T. (2006, March 8, 2006). *The Hallmarks of Economic Diplomacy for Japan: Speech by Minister of Foreign Affairs Taro Aso at the Japan National Press Club.* Retrieved May 22, 2007, 2007, from http://www.mofa.go.jp/announce/fm/aso/speech0603.html

Central-Intelligence-Agency. (2007, 15 March, 2007). *CIA World Factbook Japan.* Retrieved March 27, 2007, from https://www.cia.gov/cia/publications/factbook/geos/ja.html#People

Chen, T. M. a. L. C. (Ed.). (1995). *Common Security in Asia New Concepts of Human Security* (1st ed.). Tokyo: Tokai University Press.

Dore, R. (1997). *Japan, Internationalism and the UN* (2nd ed.). London: Routledge.

Duckitt, S. R. a. J. (Ed.). (2000). *Political Psychology: Cultural and Crosscultural Foundations* (First Edition ed.). New York: New York University Press.

Dyson, I. A. a. R. W. (2003). *FIFTY MAJOR POLITICAL THINKERS.* New York: Routledge.

Feigenblatt, O. v. (2006). *Anime as a Reflection of Japan's Development Project.*Unpublished manuscript, Bangkok.

Four Big Pollution Diseases of Japan. (2007). *Wikipedia.*

Fukuyama, F. (1992). *THE END OF HISTORY AND THE LAST MAN.* New York: The Free Press.

Glenn Hook, J. G., Christopher W. Hughes, and Hugo Dobson. (2005). *Japan's International Relations: Politics, economics and security* (2nd Edition ed.). London: Routledge.

Glenn D. Hook, J. G., Christopher W. Hughes, and Hugo Dobson. (2005). *Japan's International Relations: Politics, economics and security* (2nd Edition ed.). London: Routledge.

Greimel, H. (2007). Japan ship returns home with 508 whales *Associated Press.*

Hough, P. (2004). *Understanding Global Security.* London and New York: Routledge.

Japan, T. G. o. (1946, February 15, 2007). *THE CONSTITUTION OF JAPAN.* Retrieved April 15, 2007, from http://www.solon.org/Constitutions/Japan/English/english-Constitution.html

JICA. (2007a). Human Security and JICA. In J. I. C. Agency (Ed.): Japan International Cooperation Agency.

JICA. (2007b). *JICA Human Security- Myanmar.* Retrieved May 26, 2007, from http://www.jica.go.jp/english/about/policy/reform/human/myanmar.html

JICA. (2007c). *JICA Policies Human Security- Cambodia.* Retrieved May 26, 2007, from http://www.jica.go.jp/english/about/policy/reform/human/cambodia.html

JICA. (2007d). *JICA Policies Human Security- Thailand.* Retrieved May 26, 2007, from http://www.jica.go.jp/english/about/policy/reform/human/thai.html

JICA. (2007e). *JICA Policies Human Security Indonesia.* Retrieved May 26, 2007, from http://www.jica.go.jp/english/about/policy/reform/human/indonesia.html

JICA. (2007f). *JICA Policies Human Security Overview.* Retrieved May 26, 2007, from http://www.jica.go.jp/english/about/policy/reform/human/index.html

JICA. (2007g). *JICA Policies Human Security Viet Nam*. Retrieved May 26, 2007, from http://www.jica.go.jp/english/about/policy/reform/human/vietnam.html

Khong, S. N. M. a. Y. F. (2006). *Human Security and the UN: A Critical History* (1st Edition ed.). Indianapolis: Indiana University Press.

Koizumi, J. (2001). The International Symposium on Human Security Remark by Mr. Junichiro Koizumi Prime Minister of Japan, *The Ministry of Foreign Affairs of Japan*.

Ministry of the Environment of Japan. (2007). *Wikipedia*.

MOFA. (1999a). Development issues of developing countries and Japan's Official Development Assistance (ODA). In *Diplomatic Blue Book*. Tokyo: Japanese Ministry of Foreign Affairs.

MOFA. (1999b). Efforts toward the realization of a better global society: Overview Human Security. In *Diplomatic Bluebook 1999*. Tokyo: Japanese Ministry of Foreign Affairs.

MOFA. (1999c). ODA Country Policy toward Major Recipients, East Asia: Japanese Ministry of Foreign Affairs

MOFA. (2000a). Overview-Human Security. In *Diplomatic Blue Book 2000*. Tokyo: Japanese Ministry of Foreign Affairs.

MOFA. (2000b). Overview (The three trends in the international situation and developments in Japan's foreign policy). In *Diplomatic Blue Book 2000*. Tokyo: Japanese Ministry of Foreign Affairs.

MOFA. (2003). Japan's Official Development Assistance Charter. In E. C.-o. Bureau (Ed.): Japanese Ministry of Foreign Affairs.

MOFA. (2004). Partnership with Japanese NGOs under ODA: Japanese Ministry of Foreign Affairs

MOFA. (2005). Japan's Medium-Term Policy on Official Development Assistance: Japanese Ministry of Foreign Affairs.

MOFA. (2006a, July 28, 2006). *Assistance for "Support of Safe Motherhood in Nuba Mountains" Project in Sudan*. Retrieved March 26, 2007, from http://www.mofa.go.jp/announce/announce/2006/7/0728.html

MOFA. (2006b). Japan's Foreign Policy: Diplomatic Blue Book 2006, Efforts to Tackle Various Global Challenges to Promote Human Security. In T. M. o. F. A. o. Japan (Ed.).

MOFA. (2006c). Japan's Official Development Assistance White Paper 2006: Japan Ministry of Foreign Affairs.

MOFA. (2006d). Japan's Regional Diplomacy. In *2006 Diplomatic Bluebook* (pp. 18-55). Tokyo: Japanese Ministry of Foreign Affairs.

MOFA. (2006e). Official Development Assistance (ODA). In *Diplomatic Bluebook 2006*. Tokyo: Japanese Ministry of Foreign Affairs.

MOFA. (2006f). Overview. In *2006 Diplomatic Blue Book* (pp. 1-15). Tokyo: Japanese Ministry of Foreign Affairs.

MOFA. (2007, January 29, 2007). *Assistance for United Nations Trust Fund for Human Security project "Support to ex-poppy farmers and poor vulnerable families in border areas" Project in Myanmar*. Retrieved March 29, 2007, from http://www.mofa.go.jp/announce/announce/2007/1/0129.html

Nakasone, Y. (2002). *Japan - A State Strategy for the Twenty-First Century* (L. C. a. C. P. Hood, Trans.). New York: RoutledgeCurzon.

Olenik, W. S. M. a. J. K. (2005). *Japan: Its History and Culture* (Fourth Edition ed.). New York: McGraw-Hill Inc.

Oliver Ramsbotham, T. W. a. H. M. (2006). *Contemporary Conflict Resolution: The prevention, management and transformation of deadly conflicts* (Second Edition ed.). Cambridge: Polity Press.

Paris, R. (2001). Human Security: Paradigm Shift or Hot Air. *International Security, 26*(2).

Patcharawalai Wongboonsin, A. P., Supang Chantavanich, and Chanchutha Sookkhee (Ed.). (2006). *Promoting Human Security in APEC Countries* (First Edition ed.). Bangkok, Thailand: Institute of Asian Studies Chulalongkorn University.

Smith, P. (1997). *Japan A Reinterpretation*. New York: Random House.

Smith, P. (1998). *Japan A Reinterpretation* (First Edition ed.). New York: Random House.

Takasu, Y. (2006). "Towards Forming Friends of Human Security" On the Occasion of 8th Ministerial Meeting of The Human Security Network, Bangkok, *The Ministry of Foreign Affairs of Japan*.

Togo, K. (2005). *Japan's Foreign Policy 1945-2003: The Quest for a Proactive Policy* (Second Edition ed.). Leiden: Brill.

Trinidad, D. D. (2007). Japan's ODA at the Crossroads: Disbursement Patters of Japan's Development Assistance to Southeast Asia. *Asian Perspective 31*(2), 95-125.

United-Nations. (2001). Press Release: Plan for the Establishment of the Comission on Human Security. In U. Nations (Ed.) (Vol. 2007).

United-Nations. (2003). Human Security Now, Final Report of the Commission on Human Security: United Nations.

Wah, C. K. (2003). Japan's Renewed Focus on Human Security, *ISEAS*.

William T. Tow, R. T., and In-Taek Hyun (Ed.). (2000). *Asia's emerging regional order: Reconciling traditional and human security*. Tokyo: United Nations University Press.

BIOGRAPHY

The Hereditary Baron Otto von Feigenblatt is the eldest son of the House of Feigenblatt-Miller. He was born in the peaceful country of Costa Rica in Central America but spent much of his infancy in Spain and the United States. The House of Feigenblatt-Miller has a long history of diplomatic service during which its members have served in the civil service of five nation-states, namely, the Russian Empire, the German Empire, the Kingdom of Spain, the Republic of Panama, and the Republic of Costa Rica. Due to his family background, the Hereditary Baron was acquainted at an early age with the interesting world of foreign policy and international relations.

The Hereditary Baron attended several private international and American schools in San Jose, Costa Rica, Madrid, Spain, and Miami, Florida for both his primary and secondary education. After graduating third in his class he attended Washington and Lee University in Lexington Virginia where he studied Political Science and German Language for three semesters. Due to the September 11, 2001 terrorist attacks he was compelled to return to Costa Rica and decided to enroll in Medical School. The Hereditary Baron studied medicine for a year and a half until he was offered a full scholarship to Ritsumeikan Asia Pacific University located in Beppu, Japan. There he successfully completed a BA in Social Science after which he enrolled in the Master of Arts Program in International Development Studies at Chulalongkorn University in Thailand. Otto von Feigenblatt has participated in several international conferences and is an active member of the International Studies Association. The Hereditary Baron is currently pursuing a second Master's degree in Applied Psychology at Lynn University in Florida.

In addition to his studies, Otto von Feigenblatt, has been actively involved in the promotion of nobiliary organizations in Latin American and the United States. The Hereditary Baron is an Honorary Member of the Augustan Society in the United States and has served for many years as the president of the Association for the

Defense of the French and International Nobility for Latin America and the United States. This is an association established in France for the purpose of supporting houses in exile and the interests of the international nobility. In addition to that the Hereditary Baron is an active member of several orders of knighthood and has helped organize philanthropic events with their support.

www.ingramcontent.com/pod-product-compliance
Lightning Source LLC
Chambersburg PA
CBHW031515270326

41930CB00006B/405